D0072911

Clinician's Quick Guide to Interpersonal Psychotherapy

Myrna M. Weissman
John C. Markowitz
Gerald L. Klerman

OXFORD
UNIVERSITY PRESS

2007

OXFORD
UNIVERSITY PRESS

Oxford University Press, Inc., publishes works that further
Oxford University's objective of excellence
in research, scholarship, and education.

Oxford   New York
Auckland   Cape Town   Dar es Salaam   Hong Kong   Karachi
Kuala Lumpur   Madrid   Melbourne   Mexico City   Nairobi
New Delhi   Shanghai   Taipei   Toronto

With offices in
Argentina   Austria   Brazil   Chile   Czech Republic   France   Greece
Guatemala   Hungary   Italy   Japan   Poland   Portugal   Singapore
South Korea   Switzerland   Thailand   Turkey   Ukraine   Vietnam

Published by Oxford University Press, Inc.
198 Madison Avenue, New York, New York 10016

www.oup.com

Library of Congress Cataloging-in-Publication Data
Weissman, Myrna M.
Clinician's quick guide to interpersonal psychotherapy / Myrna M.
Weissman, John C. Markowitz, Gerald L. Klerman.
p. cm.
ISBN-13 978-0-19-530941-6
ISBN 0-19-530941-3
1. Interpersonal psychotherapy.   I. Markowitz, John C., 1954–   II.
Klerman, Gerald L., 1928–1992   III. Title.
[DNLM: 1. Psychotherapy—methods.   2. Interpersonal Relations.   3.
Mental Disorders—therapy. WM 420 W4325c 2007]
RC489.I55C555 2007
616.89'14—dc22   2006022999

9 8 7 6 5 4 3 2 1

Printed in the United States of America
on acid-free paper

Preface

This book is for busy clinicians who want to learn an evidenced-based psychotherapy, interpersonal psychotherapy (IPT), but who lack the time to read a more detailed manual or to attend a course. The book is also intended for clinicians who have had some exposure to IPT in workshops or supervision and want a reference book for their practice.

IPT was developed initially as a treatment for major depression. Numerous clinical trials support its value as such and, increasingly, with adaptations, for other psychiatric disorders as well. It has been included in official treatment guidelines in the United States, the United Kingdom, and the Netherlands. IPT manuals and clinical trials have been published for the treatment of adolescent, adult, and elderly patients with major depression; for pregnant and postpartum depressed women; for patients with dysthymic disorder and bipolar disorder; for administration in a group format, and so on. These volumes are lengthy and technical and may be impractical in everyday practice. Many clinicians have read or heard about IPT but are not sure quite what it is or how to do it. Because programs in psychiatry, psychology, social work, and other mental health professions have been slow to incorporate evidence-based psychotherapy into their training, most clinicians have not received formal training in IPT. Only in the past decade have they begun to learn IPT, primarily through postgraduate workshops or courses or by reading the Weissman, Markowitz, and Klerman (2000) manual.

We present a distillation of IPT for the practicing clinician in an easily accessible guide. Accordingly, this book forgoes material from the full manuals, such as the theoretical and empirical background of IPT and the outcome data documenting the diagnoses for which IPT works and does not work. This book is practical: It describes how to approach clinical encounters with patients, how to focus the treatment, and how to handle therapeutic difficulties. We provide clinical examples and sample therapist scripts throughout.

Section I (Chapters 1–9) describes in detail how to conduct IPT for major depressive disorder. You will need to read this section to know the basics of IPT. If you are interested in learning the adaptations of IPT for mood disorders with special populations or circumstances, proceed to

Section II (Chapters 10–17) and, for non–mood disorders, to Section III (Chapters 18–21). Section 4 deals with structured adaptations of IPT (group, conjoint, and telephone formats) some of which are also covered in earlier chapters where these modifications have been used. Section IV also addresses further training and finding IPT resources.

The chapters are relatively brief so that therapists can quickly turn to topics of interest. Each chapter on an adaptation of IPT for a particular diagnosis briefly describes the symptoms of the disorder, the specific modifications of IPT for that disorder, and the degree to which outcome data support this application. Rather than clutter the clinical text with descriptions of studies, we refer interested readers to the International Society for IPT website (http://www.interpersonalpsychotherapy.org/), which maintains a periodically updated bibliography of research. The really busy clinician should read the flow chart and proceed directly to Chapter 2, Beginning IPT.

There are limits to what a book can provide. At best, it can offer guidelines to enhance practitioners' existing skills. While this is a "how to" book, it presupposes that clinicians who use it understand the basics of psychotherapy and have experience with the target diagnoses or age group of the patients they are planning to treat. This book may complement the official manual (Weissman et al., 2000) and does not obviate the need for clinical training in IPT, including courses, and expert supervision (described in Chapter 24).

This book fills a gap in the existing clinical literature by focusing on psychotherapeutic interventions at the micro- rather than the macrolevel. It is intended for a range of mental health professionals: psychiatrists, psychologists, social workers, nurses, school counselors, as well as workers in impoverished areas where few mental health treatment options may exist.

We dedicate this book to the late Gerald L. Klerman, MD, a gifted clinical scientist who developed IPT with Dr. Weissman, his wife, and colleagues. As lead author of the original manual, he developed IPT but unfortunately did not live to see its current dissemination. We thank many colleagues throughout the years who pushed the boundaries of IPT by developing and testing adaptations. Their work is cited throughout. We also thank Carlos Blanco, MD, PhD, for his astute comments on an earlier draft of this book; Herbert Schulberg, PhD, for the case in Chapter 14; Paula Ravitz, MD, for describing her experience in IPT training in Ethiopia (Chapter 22); and Heidi Fitterling for compiling this volume.

All patient material has been altered to preserve confidentiality.

Contents

An Outline of IPT   ix

Section I   How to Conduct IPT

1 What Is IPT?   3

2 Beginning IPT   12

3 Grief   29

4 Interpersonal Disputes   37

5 Role Transitions   43

6 Interpersonal Deficits   51

7 Termination   59

8 Techniques in IPT and the Therapist's Role   63

9 Common Therapeutic Issues and Patient Questions   69

Section II   Adaptations of IPT for Mood Disorders

10 Overview of Adaptations of IPT   87

11 Maintenance Treatment of Depression   89

12 Pregnancy, Miscarriage, and Postpartum Depression   94

13 Depression in Adolescents and Children   98

14 Depression in Older Adults   104

15 Depression in Medical Patients   110

16 Dysthymic Disorder   116

17 Bipolar Disorder   123

Section III   Adaptations of IPT for Non–Mood Disorders

18 Substance Abuse   129

19 Eating Disorders   132

20 Anxiety Disorders   136

21 Borderline Personality Disorder   142

Section IV   Special Topics, Training, and Resources

22 IPT Across Cultures and in Developing Countries   149

23 Group, Conjoint, and Telephone Formats for IPT   157

24 Training and Resources   161

Appendix A Hamilton Rating Scale for Depression   163

Appendix B Interpersonal Psychotherapy Outcome
                Scale, Therapist's Version   167

References   169

Index   179

An Outline of IPT

As an acute treatment IPT has three phases: a beginning, a middle, and an end. Each phase lasts a few sessions and has specific tasks. Acute treatment may be followed by a fourth phase, namely, continuation or maintenance treatment, for which therapist and patient contract separately (see Chapter 11). Table 1.1 provides an outline of the phases and strategies of IPT or major depression presented in Chapters 1–9. Most of the adaptations follow a similar outline with adaptations indicated in each chapter.

Additional Information

Initial Sessions

Throughout these sessions, the therapist simultaneously works to establish a positive treatment alliance: listening carefully, eliciting affect, helping the patient to feel understood by identifying and normalizing feelings, and providing support, encouragement, and psychoeducation about depression.

Diagnosing Depression Review the depressive symptoms or syndrome. Assess the patient's symptoms and their severity. Use the *DSM-IV* to help the patient understand the diagnosis. Use a scale such as the Hamilton Depression Rating Scale or the Beck Depression Inventory to help the patient understand the severity and the nature of his or her symptoms. Explain what the score means, and alert the patient that you will be repeating the scale regularly to see how treatment is progressing.

Give the syndrome a name: *"You are suffering from major depression."*

Explain depression as a medical illness, and explain its treatment. Depression is an illness, a treatable illness, and not the patient's fault. Despite its symptom of hopelessness, depression has a good prognosis. You will be repeating the depression scale periodically so that both you and the patient can assess the patient's progress.

Table. I.1 IPT Outline

Therapist's Role

Be the patient's advocate (not neutral).
Be active, not passive.
Therapeutic relationship is not interpreted as transference.
Therapeutic relationship is not a friendship.

Initial Sessions

1. Diagnose the depression and its interpersonal context.
2. Define the framework and structure of treatment.
3. Provide initial symptom relief.

Intermediate Sessions

	Grief/Complicated Bereavement	Role Disputes	Role Transitions	Interpersonal Deficits
Goals	1. Facilitate the mourning process. 2. Help the patient reestablish interests and relationships.	1. Identify the dispute. 2. Explore options, and choose a plan of action. 3. Modify expectations or faulty communications to bring about a satisfactory resolution.	1. Facilitate mourning and acceptance of the loss of the old role. 2. Help the patient to regard the new role in a more positive light. 3. Help the patient restore self-esteem.	1. Reduce the patient's social isolation. 2. Encourage the patient to form new relationships.

Strategies			
Review depressive symptoms/syndrome.	Review depressive symptoms/syndrome.	Review depressive symptoms/syndrome.	Review depressive symptoms/syndrome.
Relate symptom onset to the death of the significant other.	Relate the symptom onset to an overt or covert dispute with significant other with whom the patient is currently involved.	Relate depressive symptoms to difficulty in coping with a recent life change.	Relate depressive symptoms to problems of social isolation or unfulfillment,.
Reconstruct the patient's relationship with the deceased.	Determine the stage of dispute:	Review positive and negative aspects of old and new roles.	Review past significant relationships including their negative and positive aspects.
Describe the sequence and consequences of events just prior to, during, and after the death.	1. renegotiation(calm the participants to facilitate resolution);	Explore the patient's feelings about what is lost.	Explore repetitive patterns in relationships.
Explore associated feelings (negative as well as positive).	2. impasse (increase disharmony in order to reopen negotiation) 3. dissolution (assist mourning)	Explore the patient's feelings about the change itself.	Discuss the patient's positive and negative feelings about the therapist, and encourage the patient to seek parallels in other relationships.
Once affect emerges, tolerate it in the room;	Understand how nonreciprocal role expectations relate to the dispute: *What are the issues in the dispute?*	Explore opportunities in the new role.	
		Realistically evaluate what is lost.	
		Encourage appropriate release of affect.	
		Encourage development of social support system and of new skills called for in new role.	

Table. I.1 (*continued*)

Intermediate Sessions

Grief/Complicated Bereavement	Role Disputes	Role Transitions	Interpersonal Deficits
	What are the differences in expectations and values?		
	What are the options?		
	What is the likelihood of finding alternatives?		
	What resources are available to bring about change in the relationship?		
	Are there parallels in other relationships?		
	What is the patient gaining?		
	What unspoken assumptions lie behind the patient's behavior?		
	How is the dispute being perpetuated?		

Termination Phase

1. Explicitly discuss termination.
2. Acknowledge that termination is a time of (healthy) sadness—a role transition.
3. Move toward the patient's recognition of independent competence.
4. Deal with nonresponse:
   - Minimize the patient's self-blame by blaming the treatment.
   - Emphasize alternative treatment options.
5. Assess the need for continuation/maintenance treatment.
   - Renegotiate the treatment contract.

IPT is a time-limited treatment that focuses on the relationship between interactions with other people and how the patient is feeling. You will be meeting for X weekly sessions (define the number), and the patient has a good chance of feeling better soon.

Give the patient the "sick role": *"If there are things you can't do because you're feeling depressed, that's not your fault: You're ill."* However, the patient has a responsibility to work *as* a patient to get better.

Evaluate the patient's need for medication.

Relate depression to an interpersonal context by reviewing with the patient his or her current and past interpersonal relationships. Explain their connection to the current depressive symptoms. Determine with the patient the "interpersonal inventory":

- nature of interaction with significant persons
- expectations of the patient and significant persons (differentiate them from one another and discuss whether these were fulfilled)
- satisfying and unsatisfying aspects of the relationships
- changes the patient wants in the relationships

Identify a focal problem area such as grief, role disputes, role transitions, or interpersonal deficits.

- Determine the problem area related to current depression, and set the treatment goals.
- Determine which relationship or aspect of a relationship is related to the depression and what might change in it.

Explain the IPT concepts and contract. Outline your understanding of the problem, linking illness to a life situation in a formulation:

You're suffering from depression, and that seems to have something to do with what's going on in your life. We call that (complicated bereavement, a role dispute, etc.). I suggest that we spend the next X weeks working on solving that difficult life crisis. If you can solve that problem, your depression is likely to lift as well. Does that make sense to you?

Agree on treatment goals and determine which problem area will be the focus. Obtain the patient's explicit agreement on the focus.

Describe the procedures of IPT. Focus on current issues, the need for the patient to discuss important concerns; review the patient's current interpersonal relations; discuss the practical aspects of the treatment (length, frequency, times, fees, policy for missed appointments).

Intermediate Sessions: The Problem Areas

With the patient's agreement to your formulation, you will enter the middle phase of treatment and spend all but the final few sessions working on one of the four IPT problem areas: grief, role dispute, transitions, or deficits. During this time, remember to:

- Maintain a supportive treatment alliance: Listen and sympathize
- Keep the treatment centered on the focus, as your treatment contract specified you would
- Provide psychoeducation about depression where appropriate to excuse the patient for low energy, guilt, and so on.
- Pull for affect (do not be afraid to let it linger in the room)
- Focus on interpersonal encounters and how the patient handled them:
  - what the patient felt
  - what the patient said
  - if things went well, congratulate the patient, and reinforce adaptive social functioning
  - if things went badly, sympathize and explore other options
  - in either case, link the patient's mood to the interpersonal outcome
- Role-play interpersonal options.
- Summarize the sessions at their end.
- Regularly (e.g., every 3–4 weeks) repeat the depression measure to assess symptom severity.

Termination

The third phase of IPT is the termination phase, in which the progress of the previous sessions is reviewed. Discuss with the patient what has been accomplished and what remains to be considered. Address termination several weeks before it is actually scheduled. If the patient remains symptomatic, consider another course of treatment, such as maintenance IPT, the addition of medication, a different medication, or a different kind of psychotherapy.

Section I

How to Conduct IPT

1

What Is IPT?

Overview

Interpersonal Psychotherapy (IPT) is a time-limited and specified psycho-therapy developed over a 30-year period, initially for patients with major depressive disorder but later adapted for other disorders as well. Designed for administration by experienced and trained mental health professionals, it can also be taught clinically to less trained persons. IPT has been used with and without medication (see Klerman, Weissman, Rounsaville, & Chevron, 1984; Weissman, Markowitz, and Klerman, 2000, for the full manual); a brief history of it can be found in Weissman, 2006. The primary example of IPT presented here illustrates the treatment of patients with major depressive disorder because that is its best-established and most widely employed use. The IPT approach recognizes that patients may have comorbid disorders. The approach applies to a range of age groups with major depression and to many other disorders. Adaptations for other depressive age groups and subtypes and for non–mood disorders are described in Sections 2 and 3 respectively.

Depression usually occurs in the context of a social and an interpersonal event. Some common events are:

- a marriage breaks up
- a dispute threatens an important relationship
- a spouse loses interest and has an affair
- a job is lost or in jeopardy
- a move to a new neighborhood takes place
- a loved one dies
- a promotion or demotion occurs
- a person retires
- a medical illness is diagnosed

Understanding the social and interpersonal context of the development of the depression may help to unravel the immediate reasons for the symptoms. This can be the first step in helping the patient to understand depression as an illness and to develop new ways of dealing with people and situations. Developing these new social skills can treat the current episode and reduce future vulnerability.

IPT was developed in order to specify what we thought was a set of helpful procedures commonly used in psychotherapy for depressed outpatients. We felt that defining these practices might help more therapists to use them effectively. Patients would also be better informed about what to expect. IPT has been tested in numerous clinical treatment trials for depression, in which it has been compared to psychotropic medication, to placebo, to other brief psychotherapies, and to no psychotherapy. It has also been tested in combination with medication.

IPT is one of the psychotherapies recommended for the treatment of depression in the American Psychiatric Association Guidelines and in the Guidelines for Primary Care Physicians (see http://www.psych.org/psych_pract/treatg/pg/prac_guide.cfm for details).

There are several appropriate treatments for depression. A range of effective medications and several helpful psychotherapies exists. Often these are used in combination. It is in the best interest of the depressed patient to have a variety of beneficial treatments available, but all of them must undergo scientific testing before any claims can be made on their behalf.

IPT can be an important alternative to medication for patients during some periods of life (e.g., women during childbearing or nursing; elderly people and others who are already taking multiple medications and have difficulties with side effects; depressed patients about to undergo surgery; and patients who just do not want to take medication). Psychotherapy may also particularly benefit patients who find themselves in life crises and need to resolve important decisions, such as what to do about a failing relationship or a jeopardized career. This in no way devalues the importance of medication as an antidepressant treatment. Medication may be especially helpful for patients who need rapid symptomatic relief, are severely symptomatic, have melancholic or delusional depression, who do not respond to psychotherapy, or who simply do not want to talk about their personal problems with a therapist. This eclectic view of treatment is part of the philosophy of IPT.

Concept of Depression in IPT

IPT is based on the idea that the symptoms of depression have multiple causes, genetic and environmental. Whatever the causes, however, depression does not arise in a vacuum. Depressive symptoms are usually associated with something going on in the patient's current personal life, usually in association with people they feel close to. It is useful to identify and learn how to deal with those personal problems and to understand their relationship to the onset of symptoms.

The IPT therapist views depression as having three parts:

1. *Symptoms.* The emotional, cognitive, and physical symptoms of depression include depressed and anxious mood, difficulty concentrating, indecisiveness, pessimistic outlook, guilt, sleeping and eating disturbances, loss of interest and pleasure in life, fatigue, and suicidality.
2. *Social and Interpersonal Life.* The ability to get along with other important people in the patient's life (e.g., family, friends, work associates). Social supports protect against depression, whereas social stressors increase vulnerability for depression.
3. *Personality.* There are enduring patterns with which people deal with life: how they assert themselves, express their angers and hurts, maintain their self-esteem, and whether they are shy, aggressive, inhibited, or suspicious. These interpersonal patterns may contribute to developing or maintaining depression. Depressed individuals frequently describe long-standing passivity, avoidance of confrontations, and general social risk avoidance; these depressive tactics may lead to depressing outcomes.

Some therapists begin by trying to treat a person's personality difficulties and see personality as the underlying cause of depression. The IPT therapist does not try to treat personality and, in fact, recognizes that many behaviors that appear enduring and lifelong may be a reflection of the depression itself. Patients may seem dependent, self-preoccupied, and irritable while depressed, yet when the depression lifts, these supposedly lasting traits also disappear or recede. This is the notorious clinical confusion of depressive *state* with personality *trait*.

The thrust of IPT is to try to understand the interpersonal context in which the depressive symptoms arose and how they relate to the current social and personal context. The IPT therapist looks for what is currently happening in the patient's life ("here and now" problems) rather than problems in childhood or the past.

The idea is to encourage coping with these current problems and the development of self-reliance outside of the therapeutic situation. The brief time limit of the treatment rules out any major reconstruction of personality. Many patients feel much better once their depression lifts. A time-limited, time-specified psychotherapy can help focus on goals and provide patients with the hope that they will feel better within a short period of time. Although IPT has been used for as long as three years as a maintenance treatment (Chapter 11), most psychotherapy in practice is brief. There is nothing to preclude a renegotiation of the time—adding continuation or maintenance to acute treatment—at the expiration of the acute time-specified treatment. On the other hand, if IPT has not been helpful at the end of its time-limited intervention, it may be appropriate to reconsider the treatment plan.

Genes and IPT

Progress in genetics and the neurosciences has made psychotherapy an even more important therapeutic tool in psychiatry. Psychiatric disorders are genetically complex syndromes, comparable to diabetes and hypertension, in which genes and environment are both important and interact (Caspi et al., 2003). The genotype, influenced by the environment, is expressed in the phenotype (the clinical picture).

For psychiatric disorders, the most important environment consists of close personal attachments. These connections, their availability, and their disruption (or threat of disruption) can powerfully influence the emergence of symptoms (phenotypic expression), especially in genetically vulnerable individuals. Situations in which these disruptions can be found and where symptoms may erupt have been defined as the focal problem areas in IPT. These are:

- grief (complicated bereavement)
- interpersonal role disputes
- interpersonal role transitions
- interpersonal deficits (paucity of attachments)

IPT is used with patients who develop symptoms in association with these situations. Almost any depressed patient will fall into one of the preceding four categories. Genetic vulnerability cannot be readily altered, but the environment can. Symptoms can improve with the clarification, understanding, and—especially—handling of these interpersonal situations associated with symptom onset. Psychotherapy can be crucial to this change. Evidence has shown that this paradigm works for major depression in patients of all ages and that it can be applied to some other psychiatric disorders as well. This is what IPT for depression and its adaptations are about.

Goals of IPT

The goals of IPT are:

1. to reduce the symptoms of depression (i.e., to improve sleep, appetite, energy, and general outlook on life)
2. to help the patient deal better with the people and life situations associated with the onset of symptoms.

In fact, the patient is likely to achieve both goals. If the patient can solve an important interpersonal crisis (e.g., a role transition), this not only will improve the patient's life but also should alleviate the depressive symptoms.

The IPT therapist will focus on:

- current problems
- people who are important in the patient's life at present
- helping patients to evaluate their life at this time
- the patient's affect (both positive and negative feelings)
- helping patients to master present problems by recognizing their emotional responses to those situations, using the responses to deal with them, and developing new friendships and relationships.

The IPT therapist will not:

- interpret dreams
- allow treatment to continue indefinitely
- delve into early childhood
- encourage free association
- encourage dependence on the treatment or therapist
- focus on cognitions

The patient is seen as a person in distress, suffering from an illness, and having symptoms that can be dealt with in the present.

The IPT therapist will want to know:

- when the symptoms began
- what was happening in the patient's life when they began
- the current stressors
- the people involved in these present stressors
- the disputes and disappointments
- the patient's means of coping with these problems
- the patient's strengths
- the patient's interpersonal difficulties
- whether the patient can talk about situations that produce guilt, shame, or resentment

The IPT therapist will:

- help the patient to explore options. (The therapist may offer advice and give suggestions for dealing with problems, but this is often best accomplished by asking questions that allow the patients to describe their own options.)
- provide psychoeducation and correct misinformation about depression
- help develop resources on the outside

The IPT therapist will not focus on why the patients became who they are—the goal is to find a way out of the problems, not the route in:

- childhood
- character
- psychodynamic defenses

- the origins of guilt, shame, or resentment (These are understood to be symptoms of depressive illness.)
- fantasy life or insight into the origins of the behavior

Understanding How the Depression Began

To develop an understanding of how the depressive episode began and the current context in which it arose, the patient might answer the following questions:

1. What are your problems at the moment?
2. Who are the people who are presently important to you?
   - Who are potential social supports, and from whom may you have become estranged?
3. When did you start feeling depressed, sad, blue?
4. What was going on in your life when you started to feel depressed?
   - Have any upsetting events occurred?
   - Has anyone close to you died?
5. Are you involved in disputes or disagreements with other people in your life right now?
   - How are you dealing with these disputes?
6. What are your current disappointments?
   - How are you dealing with them?
7. What situations make you feel guilty, ashamed, or angry?
8. What are your stresses?
9. What do you see as the things that you can do well? (Or were able to do well before you got depressed?)

Facts About Depression

These facts are well known to many but not all mental health professionals. There are different types of depression: major depressive disorder, dysthymic disorder (Chapter 16), and bipolar disorder (Chapter 17).

- Major depression is one of the most common psychiatric disorders, affecting 3–4% of individuals at any time.
- Depression is more common in women than in men. (This is reassuring for women patients but is not something you necessarily want to emphasize to men, who may feel diminished by hearing this.)
- Depression is otherwise an equal opportunity disorder. It occurs across countries, levels of education, and occupations. It affects rich and poor and people of all races and cultures.

- Depression is a family affair. It runs in families and has serious consequences for family life.
- Depression is occurring increasingly frequently in younger persons.
- There are many effective treatments for depression, including medications and certain psychotherapies. Sometimes these treatments are combined.
- Depression tends to be a recurrent disorder. Some patients will need treatments for long periods. Others will have one bout and never have another period of symptoms.
- No one treatment is right for all patients or all types of depression. If one treatment does not work after a sufficient time, you and the patient ought to consider another. (Indeed, if IPT has not helped after the initial time period, you and the patient should consider switching or augmenting it.)

Something to consider telling a patient:

Fleeting moments of feeling sad and blue or depressed are a normal part of the human condition. Such passing mood changes tell individuals that something is not quite right in their life. Clinical depression is different: It is persistent and impairing and includes a range of symptoms.

There are different types of depression. It helps patients to provide a precise diagnosis: major depressive disorder, minor depression, dysthymic disorder, or bipolar disorder.

Major Depressive Disorder

Major depressive disorder, the most common of the depressions, includes a sad or dysphoric mood and loss of interest or pleasure in all or almost all of one's usual activities or pastimes. This mood persists for at least several weeks and is associated with other symptoms that occur nearly every day, including disturbance in appetite (loss of or increase in appetite), changes in weight, sleep disturbance (trouble falling asleep, waking up in the middle of the night and not being able to return to sleep, waking up early in the morning and feeling dreadful), and a loss of interest and pleasure in food, sex, work, family, friends, and so on. Agitation, a sluggish feeling, a decrease in energy, feelings of worthlessness or guilt, difficulty in concentrating or thinking, thoughts of death, a feeling that life is not worth living, suicide attempts, or even suicide are other symptoms of depression. Following the *Diagnostic and Statistical Manual of Mental Disorders,* fourth edition *(DSM-IV),* patients who express at least five of nine symptoms, persisting for several weeks and resulting in an impaired ability to care for self or family or to go to work and carry out daily life, and excluding other physical causes such as hypothyroidism, meet the criteria for major depressive disorder. See Table 2.1 in the next chapter and the Hamilton Rating Scale for Depression in the Appendix.

Subtypes of Major Depressive Disorder

It has long been known that different forms of major depressive disorder exist, usually defined by particular groups of symptoms, and many subtypes have been suggested. Research studies show that the one with the most important treatment implications is delusional depression.

Delusional, or psychotic, depression includes the usual symptoms of depression, as well as distortions of thinking consistent with depressive themes such as guilt, self-blame, a feeling of inadequacy, or a belief that one is deserving of punishment. People with delusional depression may feel that the depression came on because they are bad or deserve to be depressed. Delusional depression is infrequent. When it does occur, it requires medication or electroconvulsive therapy and usually cannot be treated by any psychotherapy alone, including IPT.

Mild Depression

Many persons have mild or subsyndromal depression (e.g., symptoms such as sleep problems or loss of interest that do not reach the threshold criteria for major depressive disorder). These states are referred to by different names: minor depression; depression not otherwise specified; mixed anxiety/depression; or adjustment disorder with depressed mood. People with these milder symptoms often do not seek treatment or are seen by their family doctor, a primary-care practice, or a practitioner in a health maintenance organization (HMO) (Chapter 15). If these symptoms persist, they should not be ignored since they are impairing and can interfere with one's quality of life and productivity. Moreover, minor depressive symptoms increase the risk for developing major depressive disorder.

Dysthymic Disorder

The main feature of dysthymic disorder is a chronic disturbance of mood (i.e., sad or blue feelings, loss of interest in activities, low energy), but the symptoms are not of sufficient severity to meet the criteria for major depressive disorder. They are mild to moderate and constant. They must persist for at least 2 years to be considered dysthymic disorder but frequently last for decades. Such individuals often mistake this chronic depression for their "melancholic" personality and may not seek treatment, seeing the problem as a personality trait that cannot be changed. Yet the chronicity of dysthymic disorder sometimes makes it more debilitating than episodic major depression, and it is treatable. IPT has been adapted to these symptoms and is being tested in patients with dysthymic disorder (Markowitz, 1998; Markowitz, Kocsis, Bleiberg, Christos, & Sacks, 2005).

Bipolar Disorder

Bipolar disorder includes the presence of manic states in addition to depression. Mania is a predominant mood that is elevated (feeling high, euphoric), expansive, or irritable. This mood is accompanied by excess activity, racing thoughts, a feeling of power, excessively high self-esteem, a decreased need for sleep, distractibility, and impulsive involvement in activities that have a high potential for painful consequences, such as excessive spending or sexual activities. Bipolar disorder may also involve psychotic symptoms.

IPT has been adapted and shown benefit as an adjunct to medication for patients who have bipolar disorder (see Chapter 17). Patients with bipolar disorder require medication.

2

Beginning IPT

This chapter describes the technical aspects of how to begin IPT, including how to assess depression and complete the tasks of the first sessions. The clinician who is experienced in assessing depression can skip this section. We first describe the seven tasks to cover in the opening sessions and then explain how to carry them out. The order may vary slightly depending on the patient's clinical presentation, but by the end of the first phase the therapist should ensure that every task has been covered.

Tasks of the First Few Visits

During the first three (or, if possible, fewer) visits the IPT therapist takes a clinical history, collecting information about the patient's symptoms and current interpersonal situation. This allows the therapist to make a diagnosis and to select an interpersonal focus for the treatment. If the patient has not had a recent physical examination, and especially if the patient is over the age of 50, one may be recommended to rule out physical explanations for the symptoms (for example, hypothyroidism).

During the first visits the therapist will:

1. review the depressive symptoms and make a diagnosis
2. explain depression and the various treatment options
3. evaluate the need for medication
4. review the patient's current interpersonal world (the "interpersonal inventory") in order to diagnose the context in which the depression has arisen
5. present a formulation, linking the patient's illness to an interpersonal focus
6. make a treatment contract based on the formulation, and explain what to expect in treatment
7. give the patient the "sick role"

Reviewing the Symptoms and Making the Diagnosis

The questions in Handout 2.1 will help you to decide whether the patient has a major depressive disorder. These questions can be used as guides during an unstructured interview, can be asked precisely as stated, or can be given to a patient to complete using one of the many self-administered screening scales.

Numerous scales have been developed to measure depressive symptoms (*APA Handbook of Psychiatric Measures,* 2000). Among them, the Hamilton Rating Scale for Depression (Ham-D; Hamilton, 1960; see Appendix A) has probably been used the longest and most widely in research studies, including most studies of IPT. We present one of its several versions here as a practical example of a rating scale that clinicians can use to track the course of the depressive illness in therapy. The Ham-D does not diagnose depression but is a useful guide to help determine the degree of suffering that depressed patients experience.

The Hamilton assesses symptoms that patients have experienced over the course of the previous week. In general, a total Ham-D score of:

8 or less is considered normal, not depressed

9–12 indicates mild depression, usually not reaching the threshold of major depressive disorder

13–19 is consistent with moderate depression

20 or more indicates moderate to severe depression

30 or higher is clearly severe depression

Antidepressant medication is likely to be helpful for any elevation in depressive symptoms, but patients with scores in the high 20s or in the 30s may require medication as part of their treatment in order to ensure an optimal outcome. This is not to say that IPT will not benefit patients with such high scores, but combined treatment may be preferable to monotherapy.

Whatever scale you use, plan to repeatedly administer it to your depressed patients over the course of IPT. This helps you and the patient to measure the progress of treatment and provides helpful psychoeducation about depressive symptoms. Simply seeing them on a scale may help to convince the patient that these are symptoms, not personal flaws. The frequency with which you repeat the scale is less important than doing it regularly: for example, every three or four weeks until the patient reaches remission (Ham-D < 8).

Anxiety, Alcohol, or Drugs

The questions in Handout 2.2 and Table 2.1 can help you to decide whether the patient has problems with anxiety and/or alcohol or drugs.

Handout 2.1   Symptom Checklist

A. Depressive Symptoms

Depressed Mood

1. How have you been feeling over the past two weeks?
2. Have you felt down in the dumps? depressed? sad?
3. Have you been tearful, crying often?
4. Have these feelings gone on most of the day?
5. How long have you been feeling this way?

Diminished Interest or Pleasure

1. Have you lost interest or pleasure in most of the activities you used to enjoy?
2. Has your loss of interest or pleasure been for most of the day, nearly every day?

Weight Loss or Gain

1. Has your appetite been poor?
2. Have you lost weight? If yes, how much weight? (For how long?)
3. Have you been dieting?
4. Have you gained weight? If yes, how much weight? (For how long?)
5. Have you had an increase or decrease in appetite? If yes, nearly every day?

Insomnia or Hypersomnia (oversleeping)

For nearly every day in the past two weeks:

1. Have you had trouble sleeping?
2. Have you had problems falling asleep?
3. Have you had to take sleeping pills?
4. Have you kept waking up and feeling you had to get out of bed?
5. Have you woken up early in the morning?
6. Having you been sleeping too much?

Psychomotor Agitation or Retardation

For the past two weeks:

1. Have you been very restless?
2. Do you have to keep moving?
3. Do you feel slowed down or lethargic?
4. Are you so slowed down you have problems? Have other people noticed?

Fatigue or Loss of Energy

1. Are you tired every day?
2. Have you lost your usual energy?
3. Do you spend a lot of time in bed?
4. Do you tire easily?

Feelings of Worthlessness or Guilt

1. Do you feel you are a bad or worthless person?
2. Have you blamed yourself for things you have done?
3. Have you been down on yourself and thinking you are a bad person?
4. Do you feel like you have let your friends and family down?
5. Do you feel guilty?
6. Have you felt that you are to blame for your feelings?

Diminished Ability to Think, Concentrate, or Make Decisions

1. Do you have a problems thinking or concentrating?
2. Do you have trouble making decisions?

Recurrent Thoughts of Death or Suicide Attempts

1. Do you think about death a lot?
2. Have you felt life is not worth living?
3. Have you wished you were dead?
4. Have you had any thoughts about taking your life?
5. Do you have any plans to do so?
6. Have you actually made an attempt on your life? If yes, when and how?
7. How dangerous was the attempt?

B. Manic Symptoms

1. Have you ever had periods in your life when you were feeling very high, manic?
2. Needed less sleep?
3. Were more talkative than usual?
4. Spent much too much money or did other things impulsively because you felt so confident?
5. If yes, describe when and how.

C. Distress and Dysfunction

1. Did your (above) symptoms of depression cause you distress?
2. Did they interfere with your work?
3. Did they interfere with your social or family life?
4. If yes, describe how.

D. Medication and Medical Illness

1. Were any of your symptoms due to medications or drugs?
2. Have you been having any medical problems?

E. Bereavement

1. Did someone close to you die within the last year?
2. If yes, who? Do you feel you were able to mourn the death?

Handout 2.2   Symptom Checklist

A. Anxiety

1. Have you been feeling nervous?
2. Have you been feeling anxious?
3. Have you been feeling frightened?
4. Do you find it hard to relax?
5. Do you worry about little things?
6. Have you had sudden, unexpected attacks of panic or intense fear?
7. Are you afraid to be at home alone or go out alone?
8. Have you suffered from trembling?
9. Have you suffered from shakiness?
10. Have you suffered from sweating?
11. Have you suffered from feelings of suffocation or choking?
12. Have you suffered from butterflies or tightness in the stomach?

B. Alcohol and Drugs

1. Have you felt that you ought to cut down on your drinking or drug use?
2. Has anyone complained about your drinking or drug use?
3. Have you had to drink in the morning to steady your nerves?
4. Has your drinking or drug use interfered with work or your social or family life?
5. How many drinks do you have on a typical day?
6. If you answered yes to any of the above on drugs, which drugs have you been using?
7. How much do you use on a typical day?

Table 2.1   *DSM-IV* Criteria for Major Depression

American Psychiatric Association Diagnostic Criteria (DSM-IV) for Major Depression

A. At least five of the following symptoms are present during the same two-week period nearly every day. At least one of the symptoms is either (1) depressed mood or (2) loss of interest or pleasure.

1. Depressed mood
2. Diminished interest or pleasure in all or almost all activities, most of the day
3. Significant weight loss or weight gain when not dieting, or decrease or increase in appetite
4. Insomnia or hypersomnia (oversleeping)
5. Psychomotor agitation or retardation
6. Fatigue or loss of energy
7. Feeling of worthlessness or guilt
8. Diminished ability to think, concentrate, or make a decision
9. Recurrent thoughts of death or suicide, a suicide attempt, or a specific plan for committing suicide

B. The symptoms are not associated with a manic episode.

C. The symptoms cause distress or impairment in one's social life, work, and other functioning.

D. The symptoms are not due to the direct effects of a drug or a medical condition.

E. The symptoms are not accounted for by the death of a loved one within the past two months. Symptoms that persist for more than 2 months after a death and are characterized by marked impairment are considered depression. (American Psychiatric Association, 1994)

Explaining the Diagnosis and Various Treatments

Once you have established that the patient has the diagnosis of major depressive disorder, it is important to explain to the patient what depression is and be clinically optimistic about the future. You might say something like:

> *Depression is a treatable illness, and your chances of getting better are very good. You've said that you're feeling hopeless, but that hopelessness is a symptom of depression, not your true prognosis.*

Your clinical hopefulness does not mean that you should discount the patient's current suffering. It is also important to explain to the patient any comorbid diagnosis and how this may influence treatment.

We suggest that you first explain which of the symptoms that the patient has reported is part of the depressive diagnosis (e.g., sleep, guilt). Then educate about depression in general:

> *Depression is a common disorder. It affects 3–4% of adults at any one time. Depression may feel like a hopeless condition. Even though you are suffering now, depression does respond to treatment. The outlook for your*

recovery with treatment is excellent. There are many effective treatments available—many different medications and different psychotherapies—so you do not need to feel pessimistic even if the first one does not work.

Most people with depression recover quickly with treatment, and some recover without treatment, although that may take longer. The prognosis is good, even though some people may need continuing treatment for extended periods in order to prevent recurrence. Once you receive treatment, you should return to normal functioning when the symptoms disappear.

(Dysthymic patients may actually improve with treatment to better functioning than what they have considered "normal.")

While you are depressed you may not feel like socializing or doing the things that you usually do. You may need to explain this to your family members. However, you are going to be actively engaged in treatment and will be working hard toward recovery. The expectation is that, as you recover, you will resume your normal activities and should get back to normal, if not better. In fact, there is every reason to hope that you will be better than before, although it may be hard to believe this now, when you're feeling down and helpless and hopeless.

The underlying message is that depression is a disorder the patient does not have full control of, but from which the patient is likely to recover without serious residual damage. Treatment will hasten the recovery. Depression is *not* a failure, a punishment for past misconduct, or even a deliberate act. It is not something the patient has willed. In fact, it is important to emphasize that

- depression is a treatable medical illness
- depression is not the patient's fault
- no one wants to be depressed

However, with some patients, it may be useful to recognize that suffering from depression represents a kind of vulnerability, in the same way that having diabetes or hypertension represents other types of vulnerability.

Evaluate the Need for Medication

Although an extensive literature supports the use of medication and psychotherapy alone and in combination in the treatment of depression, empirical studies have not determined when one approach will be superior to another in an individual patient. In general, the recommendation to use medication for a particular patient depends on the severity of symptoms, the patient's preference, the history of treatment response, and medical contraindication. If the patient has severe sleep and appetite disturbance, agitation, retardation, loss of interest in life, difficulty in thinking coherently; if there are no medical contraindications; and if the burden of depressive symptoms is severe, medication should probably be recommended, either alone or in combination with psychotherapy. Since medication tends to work faster than psychotherapy, high suicide risk is a particular indication for medication—in addition to psychotherapy—for depressed patients. Indeed, high suicide risk may indicate the need for combined psychotherapy and pharmacotherapy. Pregnancy and lactation may be relative contraindications for medication. If you are not a physician, consider consulting with a psychiatrist about the need for medication with a depressed patient.

The presence of a life stress that brought on the depression does not preclude the use of medication, either with or without psychotherapy.

If the patient is already taking medication but depressive symptoms persist, IPT can be added as an augmentation strategy. Since IPT and pharmacotherapy share a medical model of depression as an illness with both biological and environmental features, IPT is neatly compatible with antidepressant medication.

Review the Patient's Current Problems in Relationship to Depression (Interpersonal Inventory)

Once you have determined that your patient has a clinical depression, you should explore what is going on in the patient's current social and family life that may be associated with the onset of the symptoms. In preparation for the immediate sessions of IPT, you and the patient will choose one (or at most two) focal interpersonal problem areas to work on. The choices, again, are *grief, role dispute, role transition,* or *interpersonal deficits.* The reason to choose a problem area is that doing so helps you and the patient to focus the therapy on the depression and the events surrounding it, rather than allowing unstructured discussion on any topic that might surface.

Review who the key people are in the patient's life to get a full picture of the patient's interpersonal connections. You will want to explore the quality of these relationships:

- How close to people does the patient get? Can the patient confide intimate feelings and express needs or disagreements?
- To whom can the patient turn for support (even if the patient has withdrawn and is not using social supports at present)?
- What beneficial and maladaptive patterns can you find in the patient's interactions with important others?

There are different ways to obtain this information, but the idea is to define the current primary problems that may be temporally and emotionally related to the onset or maintenance of depressive symptoms.

It is useful to begin with a review. Some of the following questions may be helpful:

What was going on in your life and what was happening at about the time you started feeling bad—at work, at home, with your family and friends? Had anything changed? When you started to feel depressed, what was going on in your life? Was there a disappointment in a relationship? Did your marriage begin to have problems? Were you and your children or parents in a dispute? Did your child leave home? Did you start a new job? Did someone move in with you? Did you yourself move? Was it the anniversary of someone's death? Were you put in situations where you had to meet new people and establish relationships?

These are some of the life circumstances often associated with depression. You will try to understand—and help the patient try to understand—what might have triggered the onset of this episode of depression. Even if you can find no precipitant for the depressive episode, upsetting life situations are likely consequences of the depressive episode itself. Strains in relationships (role disputes) and life changes such as ending a relationship or job (role transitions) may follow the onset of symptoms. These would still qualify as possible focal areas for IPT, inasmuch as IPT is concerned with the connection between one's life situation and mood rather than causality.

The following questions may help you to find a social and an interpersonal context for the patient's depression. These questions can be asked as part of one of the initial sessions, can be asked precisely as stated, or can be photocopied from the book and given as a self-report questionnaire before or after the session. Your aim will be to link the patient's interpersonal situation (a spouse's affair, a mother's death, a move to a different city) to the onset of symptoms in a narrative that makes sense to both the patient and you. Patient self-report forms have been developed to assess problem areas (Weissman, 2005).

Obviously these problems are not mutually exclusive, and you may find that what the patient thought was a key problem is really the tip of the iceberg. Use the initial sessions to try to ensure that you have focused on a pivotal, emotionally meaningful area for the patient and that you have ruled out surprises that might otherwise arise later in treatment. Choosing a good focus is essential to an organized and focused therapy.

The problem areas that IPT therapists focus on fall into four groups (Table 2.2):

Most depressed people have more than one problem. For the purpose of organizing the therapy and helping to treat an episode of major depression, however, you should focus on one (or at most two) during the course of the treatment. To choose multiple foci risks diluting the treatment so that there is no real focus at all. We recognize that selecting only one is not always easy, especially for clinicians without prior experience in time-limited therapies. However, our experience is that, with some practice, most clinicians are able to correctly select the main focus. Research has found that IPT therapists agree in choosing a primary focus (Markowitz et al., 2000).

1. When did your symptom *first* begin?

   _____ (Month) _____ (Year)

   Is this the first time in your life you've been depressed? Yes No

   If not, how many times have there been altogether? _____

   When was the first time?_____(Month)_____(Year)

   When was the last time?_____(Month)_____(Year)

2. Think about what was going on in your life when you started to feel depressed this time.

   Who are the important people in your life these days? Tell me about your relationships with them.

   Did someone you care about die?

   Was it the anniversary of someone's death?

   Were you thinking about someone who died?

   Were you having problems at home with your spouse or partner?

   Were you having problems with your children?

   Were you having problems with your parents?

   Were you having with your problems with your sisters and brothers?

   Were you having problems with your in-laws?

   Were you having problems at work?

   Were you having problems with friends?

   Were you having problems with others?

   Were there more arguments with family or friends?

   Were you disappointed in a love relationship?

   Did your marriage begin to have problems?

   Were you going through a divorce or separation?

   Did your children leave home?

   Did you start a new job?

   Did you lose a job?

   Did you get promoted?

   Did you retire?

   Did you move?

   Did someone move in with you?

   Did you have financial problems?

   Did you start living alone?

   Was there serious illness in your family?

   Did you become ill?

   Were you put in a situation where you had to meet new people?

   Were you lonely?

   Were you bored?

   Were there any big changes in your life?

Table 2.2   IPT Problem Areas

Problem Area	Life Situation
Grief	*Complicated bereavement* following the death of a significant other or close relative
Role dispute	*Struggle,* disagreement with spouse, lover, child, other family member, friend, or coworker
Role transition	*Life change:* graduation, a new job, leaving one's family, divorce, going away to school, a move, a new home, retirement, medical illness, immigration
Interpersonal deficits	*No acute life events:* none of the above. Paucity of attachments, loneliness, social isolation, boredom

In working on complicated grief over the death of a loved one, you may help the patient to handle role disputes with other family members, but you can still focus the overall treatment on the grief. It is preferable to keep things simple, keeping sorrow as the overarching topic, rather than to give the patient a laundry list of interpersonal problems. Sometimes the patient's problems will change over the course of treatment (particularly, of course, in the maintenance phase). For example a woman who comes in saying, "My children are my big problem" may later, as she gets to know the therapist, bring up the more pressing area of distress: her spouse's extramarital affair. (Again, it is best to try to uncover this at the start.) The idea is to identify the most recent and most disturbing stresses.

Some patients at this point will concentrate on the physical symptoms of depression, such as sleep and appetite problems, because these may feel the most distressing. They may even believe that there is no connection between their life circumstances and these symptoms, or they may either secretly or openly fear having some undetected physical illness. The latter is common and often only a fear. However, depressive symptoms can appear in the context of a variety of physical illnesses. That is why a physical examination is often needed to help in the diagnosis:

> *Over the next few weeks, we'll try to understand the interpersonal situation(s) that may be related to some of the symptoms that are making you uncomfortable. Solving those problems situations is likely to help you feel better.*

Presenting the Formulation

In the first few sessions, you will need to establish the diagnosis of depression and identify the patient's interpersonal problems. You will then tie together the depressive diagnosis and its interpersonal context in a treatment formulation, providing a potential focus for the IPT treatment.

A formulation might sound like this:

You've given me a lot of helpful information in the last two sessions; may I give you some feedback to see whether you think I understand your situation? . . . We've already established that you are suffering from an episode of major depression, which is reflected in your Hamilton Rating Scale for Depression score of 25. (As we've discussed, depression is a treatable illness and not your fault.) From what you've told me, your depression seems related to what has been going on in your life recently: namely,

- *the death of your mother, a terrible blow that you have had trouble adjusting to. We call this grief, or complicated bereavement. [or]*
- *your struggle with your husband about whether to move/have another baby/give up your career. We call this a role dispute. [or]*
- *your life has turned upside down since you moved/changed jobs/got married/got divorced/were diagnosed with leukemia. We call this a role transition. [or]*
- *your lack of friends, loneliness, or boredom. [To tell patients they have "interpersonal deficits" would likely sound insulting.]*

This kind of interpersonal situation has been shown to be associated with depression. The cause of depression is unknown and probably has multiple causes, but it is often related to life problems like the ones you've described.

What I would like to propose is that, for the next X weeks, we focus on helping you solve your [complicated bereavement/role dispute/role transition/social isolation]. If you can solve that problem, not only will your life situation improve, but your depressive symptoms are likely to improve as well. Repeated research studies have shown this to be the case. Does this plan make sense to you?

This formulation is a key juncture, the bridge between the initial phase and the rest of treatment, whose focus it determines. Choosing the focal point requires some clinical acumen. Again, the goal is to choose a plausible, simple focus based on the patient's history, an organizing narrative to which the patient can relate and which helps the patient to feel understood (Markowitz and Swartz, 1997, 2006).

Making the Treatment Contract and Explaining What to Expect

Note that the end of the formulation is a treatment contract. You ask the patients whether they agree with this formulation and are willing to work on it for the next X weeks. There are practical and financial considerations that determine the precise number of sessions we would recommend (from 12 to

16 weekly sessions). The number should be predetermined (e.g., 12 weeks)—not a range—and the aim should be to make these *consecutive* weekly sessions in order to maintain treatment momentum.

The presentation of the formulation thus constitutes a treatment contract. You may use this opportunity to explain again the relationship that often occurs between symptoms and problems in life. The patient's agreement on this focus seals the contract. You need to obtain an explicit agreement on this crucial point. Thereafter, if the patient should digress from the focus, you can bring the treatment back to this agreed-upon theme. This focal point should be seen as a collaborative effort. Although patients usually accept the presented focus, if a patient were to disagree, the therapist would explore what the patient sees as an alternative interpersonal focus and might well agree to pursue that.

The Sick Role

A second facet of the initial phase of IPT is to give the patients the "sick role," excusing them from blame for the depression and for what the depression keeps them from being able to do. It is often helpful to make analogies to other medical illnesses:

> *If you had appendicitis or the flu, you wouldn't blame yourself for being unable to perform at your best. Depression is no different.*
>
> *The symptoms of depression may prevent you from dealing with other people as successfully as usual. We will try to discover what you want and need from others and learn what alternatives there are and how to get them. We will also talk about what options are unrealistic and not possible. This is a good time to experiment with handling situations: We can discuss afterward what's gone right or gone badly. On the other hand, if you can't do certain things because you're feeling too depressed or exhausted or hopeless, that's too bad (we'd like to see how you handle such situations), but don't beat yourself up—you're not to blame for being ill. We expect that over the course of treatment you will regain the ability to do all of those things. You're fighting an illness, but it's a treatable illness.*

Having given the patient an initial understanding of how you see the problem and having reached an agreement on the focus of treatment, emphasize the following:

- *We will be focusing on your life as it is now.*
- *Therapy will focus on your relationships with important people in your life.*
- *We will discuss these relationships and your feelings. If you feel that the direction of the sessions is not useful or that I'm doing something*

that's bothering you, please let me know. I won't be offended, and your feelings are important.

Discuss the expected duration and frequency of the treatment, including how often you will be meeting. The usual time is once a week for about 50 minutes for a period of 3–4 months. Set a firm time limit, and hold to it so that both you and the patient have a timeline by which to measure progress. Depressed persons who recover from an episode but require maintenance treatment to prevent recurrence may subsequently contract to continue treatment for extended periods at a reduced session frequency.

Here are a couple of additional things to mention to the patient:

- *Anything you tell me will be kept in confidence. The only exceptions are legal ones (like child abuse or your wanting to kill someone). Otherwise, I won't talk to anyone about our treatment without your permission.*
- *In the therapy we will discuss feelings and situations that concern you and may be related to your depression. I am interested not only in what happened to you in between sessions but also in your feelings about these events. You can select the topics that are the most important to you since you are the one who knows best what things are problematic for you.*

General Procedures for Entering the Intermediate Session

Following the diagnosis, identification of the problem areas, and the establishment of the treatment contract, the work of IPT on problem areas begins. As noted earlier, problems fall into one of four areas: grief, interpersonal disputes, transitions, or (in the absence of the first three) interpersonal deficits.

It is useful to begin each session after the first one by reviewing the patient's last week. The typical question will be: *"How have things been since we last met?"*

If the patient begins by discussing mood ("I've been feeling awful"), ask about the interpersonal context: *"I'm sorry to hear that. Did anything happen this past week that might have contributed to your feeling that way?"*

And conversely, if the patient answers the initial question by reporting an event, link it to mood: *"Sorry to hear that. How did that make you feel?"*

With two questions, then, you should be able to elicit a recent incident about which the patient has feelings. The next step is to explore the incident and the patient's feelings about it. What happened? How did the patient feel about what happened? What did the patient want or expect to happen? What were the specifics of the encounter?

For example, if the patient reports a disagreement with a spouse, family member, or coworker, you would want to dissect the incident:

What did you say then?
How did [the other person] respond?
Then how did you feel?

By reconstructing such incidents, pulling for both the patient's feelings and behaviors in interpersonal situations, you gain a better understanding of how the patient's life is proceeding and how the patient is handling crucial encounters. If the patient has handled such an event well and is feeling a little better, it is important to note the connection between capable interpersonal functioning and improved mood. Moreover, you want to reinforce adaptive functioning: *"Great work! No wonder you're feeling a little better."*

If things have gone badly, as is often the case at the start of treatment, when the patient is most depressed, a similar but inverse approach applies. It is helpful for the patient to understand the connection between bad events and worsening mood and depressive symptoms. Further, it is a chance to examine what has gone wrong in the interpersonal setting and how the patient might handle a similar situation the next time it arises:

Well, that sounds painful. I'm sorry to hear about it. But let's try to figure out where things went wrong. . . . That strategy doesn't seem to be working. What other options do you have? What could you do in that situation if (as is likely) it were to happen again?

Disjunctions between the patient's feelings and actions are worth noting: If the patient felt angry but said nothing, was the feeling of anger understandable and warranted, and did that silence contribute to an unsatisfactory encounter? It's important to validate the patient's feelings, particularly negative affects such as anger or sadness that the patient may see as bad or shameful.

Having normalized these affects, what other options might the patient have for handling such a situation? Depressed patients will frequently state that they have no options for managing a situation. Feeling hopeless, they will say they've "tried everything" or that "nothing works." This is rarely true. The patient's previous efforts may have been half-hearted, and the patient may well have overlooked viable options because of discouragement, a sense that there was no reason to be upset by such a behavior, and so on. With some gentle questioning and encouragement, the therapist can often get the patient to come up with feasible options. It is best to let the patient come up with the ideas, so that the patient feels competent and can take credit for the development, rather than suggesting them yourself (which makes you look good and the patient feel incompetent).

After exploring options and finding a new, potentially feasible strategy, you can then role-play this with the patient:

What would you like to say to [that person]?
How did [the way you just said] that sound to you? Did you say what you wanted to get across? What did you think about your tone of voice?

You can repeat the role-play until the patient feels more comfortable with the intervention. The session usually ends with a summary of what has been covered and how it relates to the patient's depression.

This loosely structured sequence is the heart of the IPT intervention. The therapist focuses consistently on mood and interpersonal interaction, helping the patient to see the link between them, reinforcing adaptive interpersonal functioning and helping the patient to explore and gain comfort with new options where old strategies have not been working. Given this emphasis in the therapy, it is hardly surprising that research has shown IPT helps patients to develop better psychosocial functioning.

Involvement of Others

Although IPT is usually conducted as an individual psychotherapy, other family members may be asked to participate in one or two sessions if you and the patient feel that it would be helpful. With adolescents or children (Chapter 13), parents are always invited to participate in the initial sessions. Involvement of family members also occurs in situations of family, husband-wife, and/or parent-child disputes that have come to an impasse (see Chapter 23 on conjoint therapy).

3

Grief

Definition

Grief is selected as a problem area when the onset of the patient's symptoms is associated with the death of a significant other and the patient is having difficulties coming to terms with that loss. The significant other might be a spouse, partner, child, parent, other relative, friend, or even a dear pet. Note that in IPT, grief means complicated bereavement postmortem; other losses are defined as role transitions.

Normal Grief

Many of the symptoms that occur with the death of a loved one resemble those of depression. In a normal grief reaction, the person feels sad, may lose interest in some usual pleasures, have trouble sleeping, and have difficulty in carrying out routine tasks. These symptoms resolve in a few months, as there is a gradual weaning from remembered experiences with the loved one. The availability of family and close friends—that is, social supports—can be extremely helpful during this time. This period of grief or mourning is a normal and useful adaptation to the loss of a loved one and should not be discouraged.

Complicated Grief

Complicated grief reactions, which lead to depression, can also occur. This may happen when grief does not occur or is postponed and then experienced long after the other person has died. Sometimes it is difficult to recognize that these symptoms actually reflect the mourning of a death that occurred several years earlier. At other times, instead of sadness, patients may develop many physical symptoms or even believe that they have the same illness as the person who has died.

A complicated grief reaction may be diagnosed when grief is severe and the severe phase lasts longer than 2 months or when a loved one has died and the patient has not experienced the normal mourning process. Telltale signs are the patient's failure to mention the dead person or to discuss the circumstances around the death. Certain depressive symptoms such as excessive guilt and suicidal ideation are not usually seen in normal grief and suggest the presence of complicated grief.

The questions in Handout 3.1 can help to determine whether the patient is having a complicated grief reaction.

Signs of complicated grief can be found in patients who have suffered multiple losses and have not gone through a grieving period, who have avoided circumstances around the death such as going to the grave, who fear developing the same illness, who are trying to preserve the environment of the dead person, who lacked family or other social support during the period of bereavement, and who are still not functioning at work or with family at least 2 to 3 months after the death.

Goals in Treating a Grief Reaction

It is important to convey to the patient that complicated grief is a form of depression that can and should be treated. Treatment is not a sign of disrespect for the deceased. The goals of treating a complicated grief are:

- to facilitate mourning (catharsis)
- to (re)establish interests and relationships that can substitute for the person and the relationship that have been lost. The mourning process will be facilitated by encouraging the patient to think and feel about the loss in detail and by discussing the sequence and consequences of events prior to, during, in the immediate aftermath, and since the death.

Handout 3.2 provides open-ended questions to encourage thinking about the loss. It may be difficult for the patient to answer these questions or painful to recall details. Reviewing old picture albums, going to familiar places that evoke memories or to a place of worship (where appropriate), or calling friends or family and talking with them about the deceased can help.

Many patients fear that the power of their grief might overwhelm them. The IPT therapist's role is to encourage patients to tolerate their feelings, which feel powerful but are not as dangerous as they imagine and are likely to subside if accepted.

Some patients feel guilty about improving, seeing it as a betrayal of the deceased. They fear that if they recover from the grief (i.e., the depressive episode), it means they did not love the deceased as much as they had believed. In their way of thinking, if they really loved the person, the loss would be so great that they could never recover.

Handout 3.1   Questions to Determine a Grief Reaction

1. Has someone who was important to you died?
   If yes, how long ago? _____ (number of months or years)
2. Can you talk about the deceased person(s) with others?
3. Were you feeling sad and blue after the death?
4. Did you have trouble sleeping?
5. Could you carry on as usual?
6. Were you beyond tears?
7. Did you avoid going to the funeral or visiting the grave?
8. Did your depression begin around the time of the death?
9. Are you afraid of having the same illness as the person who died?
10. Have you left the deceased person's possessions in place?
11. Did you preserve the deceased person's possessions?
12. Were there people you could count on to help when the person died?
13. Were there people you could turn to and in whom you could confide?
14. Do you feel to blame in some way for the death? Is there something you feel you should have done—or not done?

Handout 3.2   Questions to Help the Patient to Think About the Loss

How did you learn about _____'s death?

How did you feel when you first learned about the death?

How did the person die?

What were the circumstances of the death?

When did you learn about the illness/accident?

What was the person like?

What did you do together?

What was enjoyable?

What were the problems in your relationship?

When reviewing the patient's lost relationship with the deceased person, it is common for patients to recall their pleasant times together; they usually feel most comfortable discussing these. It is also typical for patients to have felt angry, disappointed, or unhappy about some of the characteristics of the deceased and their relationship. The patient may feel abandoned by the loved one or guilty about some aspect of the relationship, particularly about something the patient did or failed to do near the time of the death. Encourage the patient to express these feelings openly since they are normal: *"No two people get along all of the time, and you must have a complex range of feelings about someone you cared so much about."*

The patient can be told that negative feelings may be followed by positive emotions and attitudes toward the loved one. This is no different from what would happen if the person were still alive: One would generally discuss upsetting things with that person, and that would make both of them feel better.

Patients with severe grief reactions may get irritated at any hints to discuss ambivalent feelings about the deceased, especially those patients with early caretaking deficits (insecure attachments) in which the deceased provided an adult secure attachment.

The patient can be told:

> *It is normal to feel upset and confused when you talk about the loss, but you will feel better again. I will be encouraging you to talk about your life with [the person], how your life has changed since, and what the ups and downs have been. I will be encouraging you to talk about the things you did not like, as well as those you did like, about the relationship.*
>
> *Gradually, you will be able to sort through these emerging feelings and build a three-dimensional picture of your relationship with [the person you lost] that includes [the person's] good and bad points, like all relationships.*
>
> *If you have difficulty in going through this grieving process, it might be helpful to discuss memories with friends or family. You might want to review picture albums or revisit places that were meaningful in your relationship. This can help you recollect the past. If you have old friends you have not seen since [the person] died, you might meet these people and review your past times together or even go over the albums with them. We can then discuss how those events go.*

Catharsis

Many patients fear that, if they begin to cry or mourn, they will not be able to stop and that the wave of grief will overwhelm them. It is important to reassure them about this. Once the patient begins to focus on the deceased person, the good and bad aspects of their relationship and of that person, the patient often begins to cry. This makes many therapists anxious and raises the temptation to interrupt the patient. *Don't do it!* Your role as therapist is to help the patient learn that *emotions, while powerful, are not dangerous.* As the feelings are expressed, their force will diminish. Patients are then likely to feel calmer and more in control—sad, but less depressed. Once patients express strong emotion about the deceased, it is important to be calmly quiet and let them talk out their feelings.

Reestablishing Interests and Relationships

Social supports are important. Later in the therapy, when you're feeling a little better, you may want to try to call or go out to dinner with a friend, just to see how it goes. Your discussion of these experiences, good and bad, and your feelings around them will be a focus of the treatment. As you begin to talk and think about the person who has died and to relive some of the experiences of the relationship and the loss, you should gradually begin to take on some of the old activities that gave you pleasure before the death. Although it may be hard to imagine this now, you may begin to look for ways to resume relationships and meet new friends that can also bring happiness to your life. We can talk about the practical efforts you are making and the feelings that surround these new steps.

If the patient undertakes a new activity or relationship, it is helpful to review afterward:

- *What did you do?*
- *What parts did you enjoy?*
- *What parts were difficult?*
- *Would you do it again?*
- *What else might you like to do?*
- *If some part of the activity was difficult, how else could you handle that in the future?*

Depressed patients who have an unresolved grief reaction may fear abandonment in new relationships. Any prospective new (or revived) relationships should be discussed, including fears about them. Similarly, discuss activities that make the patient feel comfortable and those the patient fears. Encourage the patient to risk undertaking new activities and to use the therapy to discuss experience and reactions.

As therapy progresses, the sessions will gradually shift from discussions of the deceased to issues surrounding these new efforts. The deceased person will be seen in a less emotionally charged way. Mourning continues for years: The goal of IPT is not to end mourning but to ease it and to get the patient on the right path. The patient will of course continue to remember the deceased—sometimes they view new activities as a potential betrayal of the dead—but may feel less preoccupied with the loss.

An adaptation of IPT for prolonged acute grief disorder with or without depression has been developed. This classification of grief is similar to a new category of traumatic grief. This adaptation has been used when the longing and preoccupation with the deceased are persistent. The loss of the attachment figure is seen as a traumatic loss with intrusion images. Elements of PTSD treatment have been added to IPT, including structured revision exercises, as well as motivational enhancement to help patients reengage with their life without the deceased (Shear, Frank, Houck, & Reynolds, 2005).

Case Example: A Husband's Death

Mitzi is a 56-year-old schoolteacher and the mother of two grown children. Her life collapsed when her husband, Roy, aged 60, died suddenly of a stroke. Their marriage had suffered some rockiness over finances and an extramarital affair by Roy. Nevertheless, the two were looking forward to enjoying their lives together now that their children were grown and they had finally saved enough money for vacations and relaxation. Mitzi, in her usual way, handled the funeral arrangements, comforted the children, consoled her husband's aged mother, and carried on as the backbone of the family. Her husband's death occurred near Thanksgiving, and, in the interest of family unity, she decided to continue their Thanksgiving traditions. Two weeks after Roy's death, she returned to her teaching job and began playing tennis again. She missed him and was weepy, but she felt that she had to carry on and to keep busy, both for her elderly mother-in-law and for the children.

A year later the one problem that had developed after her husband's death, her inability to get a full night's sleep, worsened. She also began to lose interest in teaching and felt that she could not go on. Convinced that she had an underlying medical problem (maybe cancer or heart disease), she consulted doctors and began to miss work. That year she was unable to carry through with Thanksgiving plans. She started to lose weight. Her friends felt she had aged 5 years in the past 12 months.

Mitzi entered IPT after a fourth medical checkup failed to find anything wrong with her physically. Her loss of sleep, weight, energy, and interest in her work and family were thought to be related to depression. Although she entered treatment, she denied that this was possible and remained convinced that she had an undetected physical illness. In the initial sessions, it was clear that she fit the criteria for a clinical depression but that she interpreted her symptoms as a physical illness. The therapist did not dispute this with her but began to inquire what was going on in her life and when her symptoms began. The therapist assessed her symptoms using the Hamilton Rating Scale for Depression (Hamilton, 1960; see Appendix A) and found that her score was 27—in the range of severe depression.

Her husband's death immediately became the focus of attention, whereupon the circumstances of his death, its sudden nature, her inability to mourn, and her immediate resumption of activities became apparent. It was also clear that her symptoms had worsened around the anniversary of Roy's death—several weeks before Thanksgiving—when her mild sleep disturbance became severe and resulted in fatigue, failure to go to work, and, finally, inability to organize the family's Thanksgiving reunion.

The therapist diagnosed major depression associated with complicated bereavement, emphasizing that depression was an illness with prominent physical as well as emotional and cognitive symptoms. Mitzi was able to agree with this diagnosis. Therapy progressed with a detailed discussion of the life she and her husband had shared. Each session began with details of her daily activities, usually a discussion of how she used to do the same things with her husband and how his loss felt to her. With the therapist's encouragement, she began to go through the picture albums of their shared life, which she had buried in a closet after Roy died. She cried frequently and acknowledged that she was really focusing on his death now, a year later, for the first time.

Over time, she revealed her anger at Roy for not taking vacations, thereby depriving them of the chance to relax and have fun together. They had now missed any chance to vacation together. Toward the end of treatment, Mitzi arrived with a brochure. She and a close female friend were planning a cruise to the Bahamas. The end of therapy included a discussion of what it would be like to be a single woman on a cruise, as well as her enthusiasm for the trip and her guilt that her husband would not be able to share this activity. Her final Hamilton Rating Scale for Depression score was 5—within the normal range.

4

Interpersonal Disputes

Definition

IPT defines an *interpersonal dispute* as a situation in which the patient and an important person in the patient's life have different expectations about their relationship. This leads to either an open or a tacit struggle.

An example is a wife who expects her spouse to take care of her financially but who has had to hold a job herself to help pay the bills. The spouse, on the other hand, may expect the wife to share the financial responsibility. This is an example of nonreciprocal expectations. Two parties have different—and conflicting—expectations of the relationship. The patient's depression can be linked to unhappiness about the balance of these expectations in the relationship, and its solution lies in their renegotiation.

Disputes are usually part of IPT when disagreements have stalled or become repetitive or stalemated, offering little hope of improvement. The parties often feel they have reached an impasse. This situation may make the patient (or both parties) feel out of control and thus threatens the relationship. Depression can make it difficult for the patient to recognize the options available to pull the relationship out of a rut or to resolve a dispute. The therapist's goals are to diagnose the seriousness of the dispute and then to help the patient to reach some resolution. A role dispute is one of the most common problem areas for depressed patients seeking outpatient treatment.

Role disputes frequently coexist with role transitions. For example, a change in job (role transition) may strain a marital relationship, causing a role dispute over responsibilities at home. Conversely, a difficult relationship with a coworker (role dispute) may lead to bad work decisions, leading to a demotion or unwise career choice (role transition). The therapist should try to focus treatment on only one problem area, depending on which one seems most important to the patient.

Goals of the Treatment

In an interpersonal dispute, the goals of the treatment are to help the patient first identify the disagreement, choose a plan of action, and finally modify communication or expectations or both so that the difference of opinion is resolved. Although the patient is likely to present the situation as impassible and impossible, some solution often exists. The therapist must help the patient to consider what options exist to attempt a renegotiation of the relationship. If renegotiation proves successful, which is the outcome in the vast majority of cases, the patient will have learned a social skill (e.g., better self-assertion, a more effective way of expressing anger to defend oneself) and resolved the conflict. Even if attempts to resolve the dispute prove unsuccessful, the patient will have learned to better communicate feelings during a disagreement. Further, the patient may come to recognize that the problem with the relationship does not lie entirely with him or her: The patient has at least tried to change things, and it may be the partner's unwillingness to change that is the problem. When the relationship cannot be successfully renegotiated, examining the options also helps the patient to decide whether staying in it is the best available alternative.

The key initial question is:

Are you having disagreements or a dispute with someone? (Is there someone important with whom you haven't been getting along?)

If so and if this dispute is distressing the patient, the next step is to determine the stage of the disagreement. The following questions will help:

Renegotiation

A renegotiation exists when the parties are in active contact about their differences.

Are you and [the other person] aware of the differences between you? Have you been trying to change things, even if unsuccessfully?

Impasse

An impasse exists when discussion between the patient and the other person has stopped. There is smoldering, low-level resentment and hopeless resignation but no attempt to renegotiate the relationship. The individuals involved may deal with each other using the "silent treatment." *"Have discussions between you and [the other person] about important issues stopped?"*

Dissolution

Dissolution may be appropriate when the relationship is irretrievably disrupted by the dispute and one or both parties actively strive to terminate it through divorce or separation, by leaving an intolerable work situation, and so on. *"Are the differences between you so large or unsolvable that you are trying to end the relationship?"*

In renegotiation, the therapist will emphasize learning new ways of communicating a solution. If the situation has reached an impasse, the therapist may attempt to bring the issues between the parties out in the open. This could result in increased disharmony, at least at first, as disagreements and disputes that have long been suppressed are brought out into the open. Argument may ensue. The objective, however, is to develop better ways of dealing with the conflict. This will help the patient understand how differences in expectations in the relationship may be related to symptoms.

In a dissolution, the patient is helped to deal with the sadness and/or guilt associated with the loss of the relationship and also with accepting it as the best available alternative. The end of the relationship becomes a role transition (Chapter 5), in which the patient must mourn the loss of the relationship and recognize opportunities in the new role.

Regardless of the phase of the dispute, it is important to help the patient realize, to the extent that it is true, the influence the patient had on the final outcome. Depressed individuals doubt they have control over their environments, yet in fact they can exercise some control. Even when the outcome is less than ideal, patients feel generally better when they recognize the result is partly due to their own efforts, rather than somebody else's.

Many depressed people have great difficulty with relationships because they tend to put the other person's needs before their own. Some patients feel selfish asserting their own needs. Anger feels like a "bad" emotion or one that will drive others away. IPT therapists validate these feelings as *normal* responses to interpersonal situations:

> *Everyone has needs, and it's important to assert them; otherwise, other people won't know what you want. If you're selfish all of the time, people don't like that, but if you never tell other people what you want or need, they may not know these things, and you are unlikely to get them. That is not fair to you and may at times create resentment for not being understood or cared for. This often spoils relationships in the long run.*
>
> *People expect others to stand up for what they want; if you don't, who will speak for you?*
>
> *Anger is a useful, normal signal that someone else is bothering you. You seem to have some reasons to feel angry. If you don't tell someone what is annoying you, that person is likely to continue doing it.*
>
> *It's particularly hard to express these feelings when you're depressed, but doing so may help to improve your situation in this dispute, and that may relieve your depression.*

The usual sequence of events is to validate patients' feelings in their description of an interpersonal encounter, then help them to put those feelings into a statement and tone of voice in order to communicate it to the other

Handout 4.1 Questions to Determine the Nature of the Dispute

The following are open-ended questions to help determine the nature of the dispute:

Whom is the disagreement or dispute with?

What is the disagreement about?

What do you see as your problems with (the other person)?

What do you want in the relationship?

What does (the other person) want?

How have you disappointed each other?

What have you done to try to solve this disagreement?

What are your remaining options? What can you do to make things better?

Are there alternatives for you?

Are there alternatives for (the other person)?

Have you considered these options or discussed them with (the other person)?

(If so, how have those discussions gone?)

How likely is change in the relationship to occur?

Could you realistically bring about the changes you would like?

How would these changes make you and (the other person) feel?

How do you usually resolve your differences?

How do you and (the other person) usually work on your differences?

What resources do you have to bring about change?

Have you had other disputes like this in the past?

Have you had other relationships similar to the one that is going on now?

Have you told the person directly how you feel? (If you did, what do you think would happen?) Could you try?

person. Negotiation requires expressing wishes directly and objecting to the excessive demands of others. If the patient reopens negotiations with the other person, a clearer understanding of the nature of the dispute emerges. The therapist will also help the patient to consider the consequences of many different alternatives before taking action.

To work out a resolution, the needs and wishes of both the patient and the other party must be heard. Sometimes in a marital dispute it is useful for the partner to also enter treatment. A separate negotiation for marital therapy might be made in which both the partner and the patient see a therapist together in conjoint marital therapy. More often, IPT of role disputes functions as a kind of unilateral marital therapy in which the patient works on the marriage with coaching from the therapist. The advantage to this approach is that, since much of the work takes place outside the office rather than in the therapist's presence, the patient can take credit for the gains achieved. This sort of "success experience" helps a patient feel mastery over a relationship situation and independent of the therapist as termination of treatment approaches.

A theme in many marital disputes is that the patient feels left out and does not share activities with the spouse. On the other hand, the patient may be making little attempt at involvement and may be expecting the partner to know what the spouse wants without being told. In these situations the therapist may blame depressive symptoms (social withdrawal, low energy, loss of pleasure) for the patient's difficulty in getting involved. The therapist will help the patient to recognize and speak clearly about specific things the patient wants (but has not been getting) from the spouse and to develop more direct and satisfactory ways of communicating with the partner. Exploring options and role-playing are key techniques for preparing the patient for such confrontations:

> *I'm interested in how you feel about these things, what you would like, and how you would like to get them. And what is [the other person's] point of view?*

At times it may be appropriate to encourage the patient to directly discuss with the partner what the patient sees as the dispute, to listen to the other side, and to describe how they talk to one another:

> *Are you reluctant to approach each other? How do you handle differences? Can you handle them in a nondestructive way?*

In the wake of such an exchange, the therapist should (1) congratulate the patient for having had the courage to risk the encounter; (2) note the link between mood shift and the handling of the interchange; (3) reinforce the adaptive maneuvers the patient used; and (4) commiserate and explore alternative options if things have not gone well.

If the patient does engage in discussions with the other person about the dispute, the following questions may be asked afterward:

- *How did you and [the other person in the dispute] communicate with each other?*

- *How did the discussion proceed?*
- *What was the outcome?*
- *What did you like about the way you handled it?*
- *What didn't seem to work?*
- *Are you glad you had the discussion?*
- *What do you see as the next step?*

Case Example: Overburdened and Unappreciated

Joan, a 42-year-old college graduate with three teenage children, recently started a new, part-time administrative job. Her depression involved a role dispute with her husband, Harry. She felt that he did not help her around the house, criticized her cooking and manner of dress, and generally made her feel terrible. Since her return to work was a response to Harry's concern of several years that she help with the finances, Joan had expected he would give her more attention. Harry had felt that they could not afford to send the children to college on one income and that a disproportionate burden had fallen on him. Joan, on the other hand, felt he had never appreciated the time and energy it took to raise the children: feeding, clothing, dressing, and transporting them, arranging play dates and recreational activities, and checking homework assignments. Since all this constituted a full-time job, outside employment would only increase her burden.

Her new part-time job, as predicted, made her feel overworked and un-appreciated. Although she had relieved financial pressure by bringing in extra income, the marital relationship deteriorated further. Their sexual relationship came to a halt, and they barely spoke to one another. Their marriage had reached an impasse. Joan felt sad, listless, and resentful around the house and argued more with her children. She started to have problems falling sleep, found herself overeating, and had gained eight pounds in the preceding 3 months. Harry, who had exacting opinions about Joan's physical appearance, then criticized her about the extra weight. Her initial Hamilton Rating Scale for Depression score was 22—moderately to severely depressed.

The therapy began with a discussion of her symptoms and their onset. It was clear that the symptoms had started after she began working and that the heart of the dispute lay in her feeling unappreciated and overworked. The therapist encouraged her to discuss these feelings with her husband, and they role-played this during a session. When Joan later broached the topic at home, the discussion resulted in far better communications in which Harry was able to express some of his own feelings of disappointments in the relationship, as well as his positive feelings about the home and the security Joan had created for him. They spontaneously planned to spend at least two nights a month together doing something just for fun. Their sexual relationship improved, and Joan's depression began to lift. By the end of the 12-week treatment, her Hamilton Rating Scale for Depression score had fallen to 7—within the normal range.

5

Role Transitions

Definition

Depression associated with transitions occurs when a person has difficulty coping with a life change that may require different behavior or modifications in one or more close relationships. The change may be immediate, as in the case of divorce or becoming a single person, or more subtle and gradual, as with the loss of freedom following the birth of a child and becoming a parent. Retirement or changes in one's social or work role—especially one that diminishes social status—are other meaningful adjustments. Moving, taking a new job, leaving home, suffering from a severe medical disorder, an alteration in economic status, a change in the family due to illness (e.g., taking on new responsibilities due to the ill health of a spouse or parent) are other examples of life transitions.

Most people do not fully enjoy such change, even when they are positive. Individuals who are vulnerable to depression may develop a depressive episode if confronted by a sufficiently disrupting or upsetting life change. Two aspects of a role transition may be upsetting. One is the loss of the old, familiar role, which may evoke a depressed nostalgia ("If only I could get back to that" or "Things were okay then") and reflect the disruption of social supports. The individual may also feel depressed and anxious about the new role, which can appear overwhelming and unpleasant. Thus the patient experiences the transition as negative. The aims of treating depression associated with a role transition are to understand what it means to the patient: what the new situation demands, what is gained, what has been lost, what expectations the person and others have in relation to that change, and how capable the person feels of meeting them.

Not all transitions are negative, but depressed patients tend to recognize the negative aspects rather than the benefits. A sought-after promotion may produce conflicts about responsibility and independence. A person may have felt more comfortable in a more subordinate position or in a less-demanding job, feel guilty about having surpassed others, or feel cut off from former colleagues whom the patient must now supervise and evaluate. Transitions may bring the loss of familiar friends or close attachments and demand new skills. Role transitions may be even more difficult if they are unexpected and undesired.

In any case, the patient is likely to recall the time before the change as idyllic, the change itself as traumatic, and the aftermath—the present—as dreadful, painful, and chaotic. This may reflect the patient's mood in the old and new roles more than the realities of the roles themselves. The therapist's goal is to help the patient not only to mourn what has been lost with the old role (e.g., being single, living in one's lifelong hometown, being healthy) but also to recognize the limitations and difficulties of that seemingly idyllic situation. Reciprocally, the therapist aims both to help the patient acknowledge what is difficult and painful about the change and the new role (e.g., being married, living in a new city, having an illness) and to recognize the potential advantages that may result from adaptation to the new role.

Some topics that the therapist might discuss to determine whether there is a problem with a transition might be recent changes in the patient's life, how they affected the patient, their feelings about the changes, what important people were left behind, and who has taken their place. Note that complicated bereavement, as discussed in the previous chapter, is really a special case of a role transition, one that involves the death of a significant other. The treatment strategies for grief and role transition are similar.

The questions in Handout 5.1 may help determine whether a transition is related to the onset of the depression.

Goals and Strategies

Five tasks help the patient manage transition problems:

- giving up the old role
- mourning the old role: expressing sadness, guilt, anger, and fears at the loss
- acquiring new skills
- developing new attachments and support groups
- recognizing the positive aspects of the new role

These tasks are often accomplished simultaneously and only gradually. They are seldom completed in the course of the IPT, but the patient may achieve meaningful successes, and you can give the patient a map for what needs to be done and how to go about it.

The therapist's first task is simply to name the role transition. Defining the problem as a *transition* rather than chaos or free fall is reassuring: As the patient adjusts to the new situation, it will become more comfortable and controllable.

The next task, evaluating the old role, explores what life was like before the transition occurred.

Handout 5.1   Questions to Determine Transitions

Have there been changes in your life recently (or since your symptoms began)?

Have you experienced a separation from a parent or other key person?

A divorce?

Are your children leaving home?

Has another person moved in with you?

Did you recently move?

Did you start school?

Did you graduate?

Did you change jobs?

Were you promoted?

Did you retire?

Have you experienced financial problems?

Have you recently started living alone?

Have you become ill?

Have you experienced any other changes?

How has that change affected you?

How has your life changed?

How have you felt about the change?

What people were left behind?

What people have taken their place?

What was life like before the change?

What were the good things?

What were the bad things?

What are the good and bad things about the new situation you're in?

Describe what it was like.

What did you used to do?

What did you enjoy?

What was difficult? How did you feel?

What else would you like to do?

What was your old [house, job, living situation, marriage] like? What was good about it? . . . What didn't you like?

Depressed patients may exaggerate the benefits of the old situation, while minimizing the negative and the extent to which the previous situation was destructive or unpleasant. Conversely, they may see their new role as entirely bad, ignoring its benefits and potential benefits. For example, a failed, unhappy marriage may be idealized because the new role of divorcee or single parent feels unacceptable. Giving up the old situation may be experienced as a loss, and a mourning process may occur. To facilitate this process it is useful to listen for and elicit feelings that the transition evokes, such as guilt and disappointment.

New Social or Work Skills

Developing new skills is an important part of the transition recovery process. The therapist is not a vocational counselor and does not assist in getting patients a different job but will help them to discover the feelings that are keeping them from adjusting to the situation and acquiring new skills, new relationships, and new friendships. It may help patients to realistically assess their assets and skills for managing the transition. Talking about practical situations (e.g., finding an apartment, learning to navigate a new community, finding a job, meeting new people) can be useful. What options does the patient have? The therapist may help the patient rehearse difficult situations, which may alleviate unrealistic fears that tend to arise when patients are depressed. Role-play provides important practice for real life.

Making the transition to the new role—the new job, the new apartment, the new home, or being a single parent—may also mean creating new friendship patterns or a support network or developing different relationships with old friends. Since the rewards to be found in the new relationships or situations are unfamiliar, they may seem less desirable at first.

In certain transitions, the patient may need to learn or exercise certain skills for the first time and may feel unprepared to perform them proficiently. Interestingly, there are positive features to be found even in objectively negative events, like a serious medical illness: Patients in IPT may come to see themselves as stronger, as survivors, with capabilities they didn't know existed, or they may learn to make the most of time, which now has an increased value in a shortened lifespan.

Case Example: A Dream Home

Jodi, a 38-year-old mother of two children, had recently moved to the suburbs and loved her new house. It was her dream: a bedroom for each of the children, an extra bathroom so that she and her husband and the children did not need to fight over the sink every morning, a sunny breakfast room, a small garden, and good local schools. Coming from a poor family who had lived in a tenement, Jodi had finally made it. She and her husband would give their family the comforts that neither of them had been able to enjoy while growing up.

They had moved into their new home a year ago. In the beginning they went through a flurry of decorating projects and adjustment to the luxurious new quarters. Over the last few months, the novelty had waned, and Jodi had started to feel almost desperate: Sad and blue, she cried often. How could she cry when she should be grateful for such splendor? Jodi felt alone and lonely. The move had entailed a significantly increased commute for her husband, the children had to travel by bus to a new school, and she didn't know the neighbors. A shy person, Jodi found it difficult to make friends. In her old neighborhood in the city, her husband had left for work at 8:00 A.M.; now he left at 6:30 A.M. and didn't return home until after 8:00 P.M.

She missed walking to the local grocery store, where everyone knew her, and meeting her old friends for coffee and a chat. She even had to give up her part-time job in the city. To keep it, Jodi would have had to commute, necessitating the expense of a second car. Her dream was collapsing, yet she didn't feel she could complain to her husband because, after all, he had done this for her and the family. She should feel grateful. She didn't relate her depression to this move; she just thought she might be overtired from the stress of moving.

A review of Jodi's daily activities showed that she spent long hours by herself in the house. The IPT therapist helped Jodi to link her depressive episode to the move. Even though it had been a positive and desired relocation, the loss of friends and decreased availability of her husband were unforeseen problems. The therapist helped her see the connection and then find new ways to meet her need for companionship. Jodi gradually became more active in the new community and discussed her feelings with her husband. Although he could not change his work schedule, he sympathized with her problems and disclosed that he, too, missed some parts of the "old life."

The IPT therapist congratulated Jodi on reconnecting with her husband and mobilizing a needed social support. Upon realizing that he shared her feelings, she felt better and grasped that she need not keep up the pretense that everything was perfect. With this improvement, she was able to make other changes in her life. She and her husband decided the expense of a second car would be worthwhile and would be paid for over time by Jodi's ability to continue her job. The car gave her a greater sense of control over her suburban environment and enabled her to drop off the kids at school. She became involved in the PTA and began to develop friends and social supports there. She emerged from twelve sessions of IPT euthymic, with a more balanced picture of suburban life. "I'm used to it now," she said happily.

Note that Jodi became estranged from her husband in the setting of her depression and this role transition. The IPT therapist could possibly have formulated the case as a role dispute but saw the marital tension as secondary to the larger picture of a role transition. The therapist also felt that the role transition would have greater plausibility and feel less threatening to Jodi than a marital role dispute. Accordingly, the therapist chose the role transition as the treatment focus but helped the patient to deal with her depression-induced withdrawal from her husband as part of treating the role transition.

Case Example: Retirement

Phil, a vigorous 67-year-old, ran a small business he and his wife had started when they first married. Over the years, they had worked together, struggled, and finally made it profitable. He eagerly awaited retirement, when he could do the things he had put on the back burner because of lack of time and money.

The previous year he had sold his store, invested his money, and planned how he would spend his time. Things did not work out as expected, however. Phil missed the daily chitchat with customers. He missed the structure of his work routine and, after a 3-month vacation, tired of traveling and wanted to return home. His wife devoted her time to cooking, gardening, their grandchildren, and volunteer work at the local hospital, but how would Phil spend his time? Over the past 2 months he had begun having trouble sleeping, lost his old zest and self-confidence, and started to lose weight. A physical exam showed him to be in good health. He even wondered what there was to look forward to. At night he took a much larger nightcap because of his insomnia and even started to drink occasionally during the day.

A review of the timing of the onset of depression and his retirement quickly led to their connection: Phil saw that the symptoms were related to his retirement and not to a general deterioration of his health. He began to discuss his work. He talked about the customers he missed, how he would have coffee every day with the storeowner next door, and his pleasure at seeing a profit at the end of each month. In later sessions he talked about the negative aspects of the work: the pressures of making payments, employee conflicts, and the demanding market.

As the therapy discussions progressed, Phil began planning to reinvolve himself in activities he had missed. He joined a golf club and volunteered in a chamber of commerce group, offering technical advice to small business owners in the community. His days became full once again, and his symptoms resolved.

Case Example: Trouble at Work

Ron is a 45-year-old accountant at a major firm in Boston. He had graduated with a degree in accounting and an MBA and joined his company at age 27, gradually working his way up to a managerial position. Over the last

6 months, his easygoing relationship with his boss seemed to deteriorate. Instead of having lunch together or informally going in and out of each other's offices, he found the boss's door remained closed. They rarely ate together. During large meetings Ron felt he was not called on to speak, and the meetings became quite formal. He believed something was going on and feared losing his job. He developed mid-insomnia, lost his appetite, became more irritable, and had more trouble concentrating and functioning at work. His Hamilton Depression score was 20. It was clear that the depressive symptoms began with the changing relationship with his boss.

During their sessions, the therapist encouraged Ron to explore and role-play options in order to help him have a discussion with the boss about his place in the company and what he might expect. Ron set up an appointment. When they met, the nature of the company's financial difficulties became apparent, and Ron gradually started looking for employment elsewhere. He realized that the dispute had nothing to do with his own performance but with the nature of the changing economic climate. The company had lost large contracts, but not any of those with which he had been involved. During the course of the therapy, Ron practiced how he would handle the negotiations with the boss. After discussing give-and-take strategies with his therapist, Ron tried them at his office and then reported to the therapist on his success or difficulty. His mood improved, and his Hamilton score fell to 11. Ron still felt somewhat anxious about his job instability but on the whole more in control of his environment. When therapy ended he had reinforced his good relationship with his boss and had made contingency plans both for staying on in the restructured company and, alternatively, for exploring opportunities elsewhere.

Case Example: Single Again

Beth, a 37-year-old mother of one, has been divorced for a year and is relieved that her marriage is over. Besides having subjected her to physical violence, her husband had neglected her and had an affair. When she finally obtained the divorce, took her 8-year-old to a new apartment and started a job, she felt that her life could begin again.

She had not anticipated, however, what it would be like to be a single mom. To whom could she turn when her child got a fever and had to stay home from school? Although her husband had never provided a great deal of support, he had at least been there. Dating again, introducing her child to unfamiliar men, and handling sex were significant stresses and sometimes defeats. In her new role as a single mother, Beth faced a life and future that seemed more than she could possibly handle. She had developed typical depressive symptoms over the past few months and had a Hamilton Rating Scale for Depression score of 24.

In IPT, Beth first discussed her marriage: the problems and issues that led to the divorce and also the early years of the marriage, including the good times when their son was born. She discussed what she missed in the relationship and concluded that it was not her former husband but the somewhat protected role of being identified as a married woman. She came to realize that she had been making all of the decisions, supporting and taking care of herself and her son for the last 7 years. She arranged for a better after-school program, which made her feel more confident about her son's well-being for the 2 hours between the end of his school day and her return from work.

Beth's major problem in the transition was dealing with new men in her life. She was afraid of making another "mistake," yet also feared being alone. In therapy she reviewed the men she had dated, her expectations, and her disappointments. Her therapist helped her to reduce the pressure she had placed on herself to find another intense relationship immediately and encouraged her to expand her social life and to include activities she enjoyed. Beth joined a tennis club and decided to take a 5-day vacation with her son and sister. In therapy, she worked on building her assertiveness in relationships with men, tolerating anger, expressing her feelings more openly, accepting that not all dates had to be successful and that it might take some time to find a stable romantic partner. Her depressive symptoms improved, and her Hamilton score declined to 9. She seemed more confident about her future and less pressured about "being alone."

Note that in the cases of both Ron and Beth, the story begins with an apparent role dispute. Role disputes and transitions frequently either coexist or lead into one another. Ron felt he was in a struggle with his boss; Beth was rebounding from a distressing marriage and divorce. Yet for both patients the principal issue was one of change—the boss was not in a personal struggle with Ron, and Beth's marriage was over. Since the key issue was the shift in their lives, rather than a struggle with someone in particular, *role transition* appears to have been the appropriate focus for the treatment.

6

Interpersonal Deficits

Definition

Interpersonal deficits, loneliness, social isolation, or a paucity of attachments may be chosen as the focus of treatment if *none of the other interpersonal problem areas exist.* In a treatment designed to address life events, this category covers those patients who present without acute life events. The somewhat confusing term "interpersonal deficits" should be understood rather to mean "none of the above"—no deaths (hence, no grief), minimal relationships (hence, no role disputes), no life changes (hence, no role transitions), and a paucity of attachments. If any of the other problem areas can be found, interpersonal deficits should not be used as a focus.

Patients treated for interpersonal deficits in IPT may have poorer outcomes than patients in other categories and might do better in an alternative treatment such as cognitive behavioral therapy (CBT) or require long-term treatment (although no data exist to support this statement). Alternatives to IPT, such as a different psychotherapy or IPT plus medication, should be considered for these patients if the initial IPT treatment does not result in symptomatic improvement.

Patients who fall into this category have few of the social supports that protect against depression, usually have impaired social skills, and feel uncomfortable in interpersonal situations. They tend to be isolated and lonely. Whereas terms such as "grief," "role dispute," and "role transition" are useful labels to describe interpersonal situations to patients, "interpersonal deficits" sounds insulting. Therapists who treat patients using this focus should state that the patients are suffering from loneliness, isolation, or a lack of attachments or supports and that this isolation is contributing to their depression. The patient's interpersonal discomfort may be apparent in the therapeutic relationship—in their difficulty in maintaining a treatment alliance.

Such people have problems establishing or sustaining intimate relationships or experienced severe disruption of important relationships as children. There are at least four types of patients who may have interpersonal deficits:

- individuals who are socially isolated, who lack relationships either with intimate friends or at work, and who have long-standing problems in developing close relationships
- individuals who have an adequate number of relationships but find them unfulfilling and have problems sustaining them (The quality of the relationships may be superficial. These people may have chronic low self-esteem despite seeming popularity or work success.)
- chronically depressed or dysthymic individuals who have lingering symptoms that have gone untreated or been inadequately treated and whose symptoms interfere with relationships (If chronic depression is the issue, it may be worth using an adaptation of IPT for dysthymic disorder; see Chapter 16.)
- individuals who have social anxiety disorder (also termed social phobia; see Chapter 21) (Patients with social phobia may want but are fearful of relationships.)

IPT is a treatment that is based on life events. This focus on interpersonal deficits differs from the others in lacking an acute focal life event. Although lack of relationships can be a major life stressor, it is often a chronic, not an acute, condition. This makes it less easy to use as a way of focusing the treatment. It is preferable to use any of the other three categories if plausible life events can be found.

Goals and Strategies

The major task in this problem area is to reduce social isolation by improving the patient's skills in spending time with and talking to people; increasing the patient's self-confidence; strengthening the patient's current relationships and activities; and helping the patient find new ones. If there are no important, meaningful relationships in the patient's life, the therapist may focus on past ones or—unusually, for IPT—on the relationship with the therapist. The purpose of this is to help patients understand their problems in relationships and to practice forming new relationships.

The three tasks involved are:

- to review past significant relationships, both good and bad
- to explore patterns of strengths and difficulties in these relationships
- to discuss the patient's feelings, both positive and negative, about any current relationships (including possibly that with the therapist)

The therapist will want to know about current friends and family:

- *How often do you see them?*
- *What do you enjoy about seeing them?*

- *What problems come up?*
- *How can you find friends and activities like those you used to enjoy in the past or new ones that you might enjoy?*

The therapist should anticipate difficulties in the therapeutic treatment with patients:

You have said it's hard for you to feel comfortable around other people. I expect that may happen here. If you feel shy and it's uncomfortable to talk to me, you can tell me so. If I should happen to do anything that annoys you, please bring it up. I won't be trying to bother you, but it's exactly that kind of tension between people we should be talking about and deciding how you can handle. Learning to talk openly about feelings in therapy may make it clear that your feelings, both positive and negative, aren't so dangerous to bring up, and that might make it easier for you in other relationships.

You might encourage the patient to work on isolation between sessions by recontacting old friends (or possibly new ones) and seeking out social situations.

Therapy is a great time to work on your relationships; we can talk about what goes right or wrong.

You and the patient can anticipate potential problems and how they might be handled, then discuss afterward how the contact actually went. No formal homework should be prescribed since patients who do not comply with homework tend to feel like "bad" patients and may be more likely to drop out of treatment. Role-play of difficult anticipated situations is often helpful and reassuring to patients. Indeed, patients in this category are likely to need considerable role-play before developing social confidence.

If the patient contacted an old friend and arranged to see that person, you can ask:

Describe how it went. How did you feel? What did you say? . . . Then what happened? Then how did you feel? What did you say?

Each described encounter provides an opportunity for you to validate the patient's feelings, reinforce positive actions that the patient has taken, offer solace, encourage exploration of alternative options, and then role-play those alternatives for interactions that have not gone well. Each reconstruction of an interpersonal encounter also offers an opportunity to note differences between what the patient felt and what depression may have held the patient back from saying. The IPT therapist can frequently validate the patient's feelings and then encourage the patient to express them:

Was your feeling angry when he said that a reasonable feeling? . . . If so, how might you express that? (Or: What would you think about just saying to him what you just said to me now?)

Handout 6.1   Questions to Determine Available Relationships

Tell me about your relationships. Are there people you feel close to?

  Do you currently have

- friends?
- a lover?
- contacts with family members?

Do you find it difficult to keep close relationships once you make them?

What makes it hard?

Do you enjoy close relationships when you have them?

Do you have problems making close relationships?

How often each month do you see your close friends? _____ times

How often each month do you see your family? _____ times

_____

_____

_____

_____

_____

_____

_____

_____

_____

_____

_____

_____

_____

_____

Handout 6.2   Questions to Determine Relationship Patterns

The following questions might help to explore the patient's patterns of getting along with others:

Describe how you meet people. (Or: What makes it hard to meet people?)

How do you begin conversations?

Do you have problems knowing what do in a relationship once you go beyond first meeting a new person?

What happens when you are with friends?

What kind of activities do you like to do with friends?

How does your relationship with friends make you feel?

How do you get along with your family members?

What happens when you disagree about something?

Is it hard for you to tell people when they're annoying or frustrating you?

Can you tell people when you need or want things?

Pretend you are in a room full of strangers at a party. Describe what you would do to meet people:

_____

_____

_____

_____

_____

_____

_____

_____

_____

_____

If the patient arranged to enter a social situation, a party, a concert, sports, or any type of situation, you can say:

Describe how it went. What did you do to meet people? How did you feel?

Interpersonal difficulties are usually worsened by depression and—more to the point in IPT—may be a reflection of depression. The clinician should determine whether the deficits are chronic or acute and just a consequence of the (possibly chronic) depression. Depressed patients lack the energy and confidence to pursue relationships. It is important *not* to assume that the patient has a personality disorder when seen in the midst of a depressive episode since apparent personality "traits" may wane or vanish with treatment of the depression. The goal is to reduce social isolation and improve current relationships by improving skills in communicating and increasing the patient's social competence and confidence.

Case Example: "I Can't Make Friends"

Diane, a 23-year-old single woman, had never been socially comfortable, but she had managed to fit in and make the best of it with friends she had known for years in high school, while living in a single-sex dormitory in college, and in planned school activities. She avoided dating in school. Now she was on her own. In the year since she graduated from college she had found her first job and gotten her own apartment. Yet she felt at a loss.

Even though Diane had a good job that she had planned and studied for, she could not deal with her discomfort around men. She did not know how to talk to them, how to develop friendships, how to extricate herself from relationships that were uncomfortable, and how to avoid sexual involvement with men she hardly knew or liked. She spent most of her time after work alone in her apartment. Her attempts to develop new friendships were disastrous. She went to a dance and became sexually involved with someone she hardly knew or liked. She described herself as bored and lonely. She had lost weight, was having trouble sleeping, and had missed several days at work. Her therapist defined her problem as major depression related to role deficits in social skills.

Therapy began with a detailed discussion of her daily activities—how Diane spent each day at work, her evenings, and the weekends. Therapist and patient also reviewed how her college relationships had developed since she graduated, finding a clear pattern of increasing withdrawal after her first, unsuccessful efforts to find friends when she had moved to town. She was very shy, felt unattractive and awkward, and did not know how to start a conversation or how to set boundaries in relationships.

On the positive side, Diane was a reasonably good athlete and had excelled in swimming in college, where she had one "best friend." The therapist encouraged her to act on her idea to invite the friend for a weekend, then to gradually increase her social activities with another trusted friend. Therapy included discussions of these opportunities and her anxieties and role-playing with the therapist—planning the weekend with her friend, approaching people at the swimming club she joined, and warding off premature sexual advances from men she barely knew or did not like.

Diane made some progress in doing so. By the end of therapy her depressive symptoms had decreased from the moderate to the mild range, she had bolstered her relationships with women friends, and she had successfully turned aside one unwanted man. She had yet, however, to begin dating comfortably or seriously. Patient and therapist agreed to a 1-year maintenance course of monthly IPT (see Chapter 11) in order to build upon and further the gains Diane had made acutely.

Note Although Diane has what could be termed interpersonal deficits, another way to formulate this case might have been as a role transition—namely, the transition out of college and into adulthood. A key aspect of this shift would have been the need to adjust to social relationships. This might have been a more palatable formulation for a sensitive patient than the isolation/paucity of relationships rubric. The IPT formulation is intended to simplify problems and make them manageable so that the exploration of affect and interpersonal skill building can take place (Markowitz & Swartz, 1997; in press).

Case Example: "The Relationships Never Last"

Bill was an attractive 41-year-old lawyer. He had been briefly married in his twenties, had a moderately successful career, and reported a series of relationships with women that never lasted more than 4 to 6 months. After the date—dinner, dancing, or a movie—he felt socially awkward and did not know how to get close to women. He described himself as sexually uninterested because he had not yet met the right woman, but further disclosure showed that he had low self-esteem and felt completely at a loss with regard to emotional intimacy. He felt unable to make a woman understand what kind of person he was, how to talk about himself, or how to encourage a woman talk about herself.

In treatment with a female therapist, it was clear that he had a great deal of difficulty talking about his feelings. He confided in no one, even though he said he had several close friends. He wanted to marry and have children. He felt that he was getting older and more set in his ways and that this problem was becoming more difficult. In the last several months, following the breakup of his last relationship with Janet, who stopped answering his phone calls, he found himself increasingly depressed. His initial Hamilton Rating Scale for Depression score was 23.

With Bill, IPT included exploring his feelings about interpersonal encounters, voicing these feelings in therapy, receiving validation from the therapist (who normalized much of what he felt and attributed some of his excessive anxiety to depression), and practicing relationships (role-playing). The therapist and Bill role-played his being in a relationship with somebody he knew well, practicing what he might say and how he might reveal his feelings or get the person to talk about herself. A clear pattern emerged from these practice sessions. He never let the other person finish a sentence but instead jumped in to lecture them, thus closing off further discussion. He came across as judgmental and controlling.

When the therapist pointed this out, Bill said that this was exactly how he would describe his own mother. In fact, last week they had had a major argument. When Bill had told his mother about his relationship with Janet, his mother had responded with a lecture about his clothes, his manners, and his work schedule. He became infuriated, they argued, and he slammed down the telephone. Communication ceased, and he could discuss neither his disappointment at the breakup of the relationship nor his anger at his mother. In IPT, as he discussed other relationships and how they had ended, he gradually became aware of his possible contribution to them. The therapeutic relationship provided a here-and-now laboratory for listening, gauging his feelings, speaking to another person, and gauging her feelings.

By the end of treatment he had not found a steady relationship but had become more aware of his feelings and his behaviors through therapy and was socializing somewhat more. He had confronted his mother about her lecturing, finished that conversation, and gotten her to back off. He was learning to listen to other people rather than interrupting out of anxiety. As he did so, his mood gradually improved, and his Hamilton score at termination was 10 (mildly depressed).

7

Termination

IPT is a time-limited, not an open-ended, treatment. The time selected can vary: In IPT studies the interval has been as brief as 6 weekly sessions and as long as 36 monthly sessions. The sessions usually run 12–16 weeks for treatment of acute major depression. At the beginning, therapist and patient make an explicit contract about the frequency and length of the treatment. Several sessions before the end of the agreed-upon interval, the therapist begins an open discussion about the end of the treatment and reviews what has been accomplished and what remains to be done. The patient should be encouraged to discuss any feelings about ending the therapy.

The therapist emphasizes that the goal of the treatment has been to treat the depression and to help the patient deal successfully with life: work, love, and outside friendships. The patient-therapist relationship is a temporary one meant to enhance the patient's health, not to substitute for real-world relationships.

The goals of the termination phase are:

- to conclude the acute treatment with the recognition that separations are role transitions and hence may be bittersweet but that the sadness of separation is not the same thing as depression
- to bolster the patient's sense of independence and competence, if treatment is to end
- to relieve guilt and self-blame if the treatment has not been successful and to explore alternative treatment options
- to discuss continuation or maintenance treatment if IPT has been acutely successful but the patient is at high risk for relapse or recurrence (If the patient is still symptomatic, it is also time to consider medication as an additional or solo treatment. If the patient has not received medication, a therapist who is not a physician may want a psychiatric consultation if the patient is still having sleep and appetite problems and low energy and/or expresses suicidal thoughts)

Most patients have some discomfort with termination. A degree of sadness should be acknowledged as normal: You have been working on intimate matters together, it's been hard work, and it's hard to break up a good team. Indeed, the distinction between sadness and depression is a helpful one: Sadness is a normal signal of interpersonal separation and does not mean the patient's depression is returning. Moreover, some patients, even if greatly improved, may have been feeling better for a matter of only weeks and may still feel somewhat shaky about handling matters on their own—without the therapist.

If a patient does not want to terminate, the therapist often suggests a waiting period of several months to see whether further treatment is really needed. Exceptions to this can be made if the patient has a significant burden of residual symptoms or has shown little or no improvement in the depression. In such cases, discussion should include consideration of alternative treatments, including adding or changing medication or switching to a different type of psychotherapy; psychotherapy with a different therapist; or renegotiation of the contract with the current therapist. In cases in which there have been additional changes in the patient's environment during the therapy (e.g., the unexpected death of a loved one during the treatment of a role transition), it may be appropriate to extend the therapy for a few additional sessions.

Depressed patients enter treatment feeling disorganized and incompetent. Many patients will improve in IPT treatment, but even so they may feel anxious about stopping treatment because they recall that only a few weeks before they felt very depressed. The therapist should help the patient terminate the IPT feeling organized and competent. One way to accomplish this is to review the patient's depressive symptoms (e.g., with the use of the Hamilton Rating Scale for Depression), note the great improvement (or achievement of remission [Ham-D < 8]), and then ask the patient: "*Why have you gotten better?*"

Patients tend to credit therapists for their gains, but in IPT the focus on the patient's activity outside the therapy office usually makes it clear that the patient has also done hard work and that the success is the result of their collaborative effort. Termination is an opportunity to give patients credit for their own gains by reviewing their new strengths, noting how their use of new skills was associated with symptomatic improvement and anticipating how they can use these skills to face upcoming situations. In short, the patient may not need the therapist any longer at this point, although the patient is always encouraged to seek help again if symptoms return.

Some patients may require longer-term treatment or maintenance IPT to prevent relapse or recurrence. This includes patients with a history of recurrent depression: The more depressive episodes a patient has, the more episodes are likely to occur. Another high-risk group comprises patients who have responded to treatment but still have high levels of residual symptoms. For example, a patient whose Hamilton Rating Scale for Depression score has decreased from 30 at intake to 13 after 12 sessions has certainly responded to IPT, but a score of 13 remains symptomatic and near the threshold for depressive relapse.

Some patients with recurrent depression that has resolved during 12–16 weeks of acute IPT will do well and have a reduced risk of relapse or recurrence with monthly maintenance IPT. If maintenance treatment seems indicated, a new treatment contract should be made (see Chapter 11). Monthly maintenance IPT is the best-tested interval, but some patients may want and benefit from more- or less-frequent sessions. The patient's preference for the frequency of such sessions may be an important consideration: Some patients may want to meet every 2 weeks, whereas others may find such frequent meetings burdensome in their euthymic state.

Patients who have not responded to IPT and who remain symptomatic should be evaluated for medication and/or a different type of psychotherapy. Nearly all depressions respond to treatment, and 12–16 weeks is already a long time to wait for treatment response. A risk of ineffective treatment is that the depressed patients are likely to blame themselves ("This is supposed to be a great treatment, but I'm a failure") and may become too discouraged to persevere in treatment. If the patient has not improved, the IPT therapist invokes the medical model and—as the therapist would do in a pharmacological treatment—blames the treatment, not the patient, for nonresponse. The patient can be given the example that only two-thirds of patients with major depression respond to their first course of pharmacological treatment. Yet the majority of those nonresponders will likely respond to a subsequent course of treatment. The goal of this discussion is to consider therapeutic options and to find a more effective treatment to alleviate the patient's pain. Some patients who have been initially unwilling to take medication may have built a sufficient alliance during an unsuccessful IPT treatment to now willingly consider a pharmacology trial. In that sense, even a failed IPT trial could lead to a success.

There is a good chance that the patient will not be depressed at the end of treatment. This improvement should be acknowledged and the patient congratulated for having accomplished something that probably seemed very unlikely only weeks before. It may take a while for the patient to feel secure that the depression is truly gone and will not come back. The patient should be told that the symptoms of depression and the kinds of interpersonal situations likely to be associated with the depression may recur. The therapist should encourage patients by pointing out that they may be able to handle moods and situations differently when they occur and avoid a relapse or recurrence. If the symptoms do return, the patient should know whom to contact and how to get help quickly, including contacting the IPT therapist again. Such a relapse or recurrence should not be seen as a failure on the patient's part but rather as a reappearance of a chronic vulnerability to illness, akin to hypertension or high cholesterol.

At the end of treatment the clinician should repeat the depression and other diagnostic assessments to evaluate the progress in a concrete way. To see how much progress has been made on the problem areas or whether new problems have developed, the problem area questions on grief, disputes, transitions, or deficits, which were asked at the beginning of treatment, might be readministered and the results discussed with the patient. See Appendix B for an Interpersonal Psychotherapy Outcome Scale, Therapist's Version, which may help guide the evaluation of progress in the problem areas (Markowitz, Bleiberg, Christos, & Levitan, 2006).

8

Techniques in IPT and the Therapist's Role

The strategies used in IPT as described in the preceding chapters are distinctive. On the other hand, the techniques used to facilitate these strategies are neither unique nor new; most of them will be familiar to any experienced psychotherapist clinician. Some of these methods have been more explicitly stated from a patient's point of view in the patient handbook (Weissman, 2005). The time spent in therapy is used to discuss feelings and take action to change in kind or in perception the patient's feelings in the identified problem area. The following techniques are used to accomplish this.

Nondirective Exploration

Nondirective exploration uses open-ended questions to facilitate free discussion in order to gain information and identify problem areas. Here are some examples of questions:

> *Who are the important people in your life? How have you been since we last met?*

With a supportive acknowledgement, the therapist encourages the patient to continue: *"Please go on," "I understand,"* or, to deepen or extend the topic, *"Can you tell me more about the friend you mentioned earlier?"* Nondirective exploration is useful with a verbal patient to focus the treatment, but it can make a nonverbal patient anxious. Since the therapeutic goal is to develop a comfortable alliance, more directed, active techniques are indicated for the nonverbal patient.

Direct Elicitation

Direct elicitation of material is used to obtain specific information, for example, to develop the interpersonal inventory, to obtain symptoms in order to make a diagnosis, or where specific information is needed to demonstrate a point, such as defining a patient's role in a dispute or an unexpressed af-fect. For example: *"Can you tell me what you said before your wife accused you?"* and *"How did you feel when clearing out your husband's clothes after the funeral?"*

Encouragement of Affect

Encouragement of affect is used to help the patient express, understand, and manage affect. The expression of affect may help the patient decide what is important and to make emotionally meaningful changes. Choosing options and making changes are more difficult if patients do not fully recognize the range and intensity of their feelings about key interpersonal situations. Pa-tients may not be aware of their sense of guilt, anger, or sadness, and their expression may help to clarify and point in a direction.

One way to help the patient deal with and accept painful affect, espe-cially in grief reactions, is to elicit details of the patient's interactions with others or to explore topics to which a patient has shown an emotional re-sponse. In the case example of Mitzi in Chapter 3, "A Husband's Death," the patient had idealized her husband and was able in therapy to express some of her disappointment and the burden she experienced with his ill-ness. In the case example of Phil in Chapter 5, "Retirement," the direct exploration of the patient's interactions at work allowed him to begin to make the transition into the retirement he had previously accepted with reluctance. Patients who often feel guilty about expressing negative feel-ings may benefit from direct reassurance such as *"Most people would feel like that"* or *"It makes sense to feel angry."* This conveys the therapist's acceptance of the patient's feelings.

Although patients can be encouraged to express their emotions within the therapy, this is not necessarily how they should act in close interper-sonal relationships outside of treatment. Strong expression of anger and re-sentment might damage already fragile relationships. The first steps are to elicit the feelings in the therapeutic situation, to normalize them where possible, and then to discuss the pros and cons of expressing them or how best to express them in existing relationships. When possible, the therapist can encourage the patient to use social supports to express feelings. How-ever, how best to do so, to whom, and what reactions can be anticipated are options to explore and to role-play in IPT before the patient tries them out at home or work.

If some of the behavior or circumstances of the troubling problem change, some of the patient's angry affect may also be reduced. Not only can the IPT therapist encourage angry and resentful feelings, but many patients have dif-ficulty expressing affection, gratitude, or caring and can learn to express these both in the therapy hour and within outside relationships. Listen for emo-tionally important statements, and encourage an expansion by discussing

them. On the other hand, constant repetition of angry, hostile, and sad out-
bursts can be counterproductive. When this occurs, the therapist can help
the patient to explore other options to break a maladaptive pattern of emotional expression. For example:

> *You seem to get into this pattern that doesn't really help you to feel better.
> Do you agree? . . . What other options might you have to express these
> feelings? How else might you communicate how you feel to your friend?*

Alternatively, an excessively affective display may be diminished by in-
quiring about the patient's thoughts about these strong feelings and exploring how the patient may delay acting on an impulse, allowing time to consider
the consequences.

Clarification

Asking a patient to clarify a statement is a useful technique to make the patient more aware of what is being communicated. Patients can be asked to
repeat or rephrase what they said. The therapist may then rephrase this by
saying, *"You were angry with her?"* The therapist may call attention to the
logical extension of a statement the patient has made: *"Do you mean to say
that you would like your daughter to move out of the house?"*

Contradictions and contrasts can be brought to the patient's attention.
For example, *"You just described your husband's affair without showing any
emotion. How do you feel about this?"* or *"You were smiling when you told me
about the angry exchange between you and your friend."* This can be handled
by saying, *"I noticed that you said X when you had previously said something
else."* Or, *"Before, when you told me about this, you were sad, and now you seem
to be calm."*

Communication Analysis

Communication analysis is used to examine and identify problems in communication in order to help patients more effectively deal with their significant other. The therapist elicits a detailed account of an important
conversation or argument that the patient has had with a significant other
for several purposes: to understand the meaning of the transaction, as well as
the pair's methods of communication. The therapist listens to the communication in detail, stopping to understand the patient's feelings and intents
at critical points: *"Then what did you say? . . . Then how did you feel?"* Am-
biguous, indirect, nonverbal communication can be identified as a less than
satisfactory alternative to verbal confrontation (e.g., the patient who sulks
when angry). Patients are often not aware of how they communicate or how

their depression may distort other people's messages. Communication analysis may help them detect these difficulties in communication and allow for their correction. At the same time, when treating patients from other cultures, it is important to take into account which forms of communication are accepted and which are proscribed in the patients' culture. Although therapists may be tempted to use their own culture as a referent, adopting the therapist's modes of communication might not always be in the patient's best interest (see Chapter 22).

Another technique is to communicate directly about one's needs and feelings. Many patients assume that others will anticipate their wants or read their mind, which can result in anger, frustration, silence, and unexpressed affect that can destabilize a relationship.

Incorrect assumptions that one has been understood also need to be clarified. For example, was a statement a friend made about the patient's hair meant as a criticism or a compliment? To identify faulty communication, listen for assumptions that patients make about others' thoughts or feelings. Rather than giving immediate feedback, encourage patients to draw their own conclusions. Follow through a particular conversation, again checking patients' feelings as you progress. After they have offered their interpretation of events, you can elicit and suggest alternatives to poor communication and use role-play (see below) to help improve communication.

Decision Analysis

This technique helps the patient to consider alternative courses of action and their consequences in order to solve a given problem. Like most IPT techniques, the patient can learn to use it not only within the treatment but also as a general interpersonal skill. Questions such as *"What would you want to happen?" "What solution to this would make you happiest?" "What are the alternatives?"* and *"Have you considered all the choices?"* may be helpful.

Role-Play

Role-play can be useful across the four IPT problem areas. Especially for patients who have interpersonal deficits, it can be useful for them to take the role of some person in their life with whom they would like to develop a relationship, Role-play can help prepare them to interact with others in different ways, particularly in being more assertive or expressing anger, and also to obtain information on how they react to others. In other cases (e.g., role disputes or role transitions), role-play may helpfully rehearse the patient's handling of new situations or new ways to handle old situations. In instances of grief, it is often useful to role-play an imaginary conversation between the patient and the deceased person.

The Therapeutic Relationship

IPT does not exploit or interpret the transference that occurs in longer-term psychotherapies or in short-term psychodynamic psychotherapy in which the transference is an essential part of the treatment. However, the therapist does pay attention to the therapeutic relationship, recognizing that this may reflect how the patient thinks and acts in other close relationships. Although the focus of treatment remains squarely outside the office, rather than on the therapeutic dyad, the therapist can ask the patient to express negative feelings about both the therapy and the therapist, as well as to voice complaints, apprehensions, anger, and aversive feelings that may arise in the course of the treatment. These exchanges focus on the here-and-now interpersonal issues, not on childhood antecedents or other remote historical material. They allow the therapist to correct distortions or acknowledge genuine deficiencies or problems in the treatment. (IPT therapists need not hesitate to apologize for mistakes they may make.) This approach also helps patients to feel understood by the therapist and to see themselves as a partner in the treatment process.

The therapeutic relationship can be used in role disputes to give feedback on how the patient comes across to others and to help the patient understand maladaptive approaches to interactions. In interpersonal deficits, the patient's relationship with the therapist may provide a model for interacting in other relationships. Directive techniques include interventions such as educating, advising, modeling, or directly helping the patient solve relatively simple, practical problems such as referrals for social service, housing, public assistance, medical insurance, or educational opportunities for family members. Advice, suggestions, limit setting, education, direct help, or modeling are elements of the therapeutic relationship but not necessarily a major part of it. They are best employed in early sessions to create an atmosphere in which the therapist is perceived as helpful. Advice should ideally take the form of helping the patient to consider options not previously entertained (rather than direct suggestion).

The Therapist's Role

The therapist's stance is that of a friendly, helpful ally, evoking what would be expected of any physician, nurse, or other health professional. The therapist needs of course to draw boundaries when necessary: Being warm and friendly does not mean having a social friendship. Self-disclosure can be effective in rare circumstances but is generally discouraged. The focus should be on the patient, not on indulging the therapist's needs. IPT is an active therapy, and therapists should not allow long, painful silences. On the other hand, too much therapist activity can fragment patient affect, keeping sessions from building the depth of emotion that can make therapy effective. It takes practice to balance activity and reflective listening. Keeping interventions pithy—using a minimum of words—tends to maximize effectiveness. Patients with poor concentration can get lost in long speeches, which tend to intellectualize the treatment.

In summary:

- The therapist is the patient's advocate and is not neutral. If the patient is self-deprecating, IPT therapists attribute such remarks to being depressed. Depressed patients are likely to take the therapist's silence after such self-criticism as agreement that the patient is worthless or as a withholding behavior on the therapist's part. Being the patient's advocate does not mean doing things for the patient. Rather, it means trying to understand things from the patients' point of view and validating it (aside from the depressive outlook), siding with them against a sometimes hostile environment and encouraging them to do things that they are capable of doing to change that environment.
- The therapist attempts to be nonjudgmental. Yet encouraging change in behaviors the therapist believes wrong, such as antisocial behavior, is a judgment and should be acknowledged as such.
- The therapeutic relationship is not viewed in terms of transference. The patient's expectations of assistance and understanding from the therapist are realistic and are not to be interpreted as a reenactment of the patient's previous relationships with others. The assistance that IPT therapists offer is limited to helping patients to learn and test new ways of thinking about themselves and their social roles and solving interpersonal problems. When difficulties arise in the therapeutic relationship (e.g., the patient becomes angry at or feels criticized by the therapist), these are addressed in here-and-now, interpersonal fashion:
  - *Let's talk about what's going on between us. It's good that you're telling me you're upset—this is the sort of interpersonal communication we're working on, and with your feedback I can stop doing what's bothering you.*

Limits are set the same way they would be in relationships with other medical clinicians.

- The therapist is active, not passive. The therapist actively helps focus on improving the patient's current situation.
- The therapist encourages the patient to think of solutions to interpersonal problems. If the patient is unable to come up with new approaches, despite probing or leading questions from the therapist, then the therapist may suggest alternatives.

9

Common Therapeutic Issues and Patient Questions

This section includes some therapeutic issues that commonly arise when therapists begin practicing IPT. Also considered are common patient concerns and ways to handle them in IPT. Psychotherapy is not a normal experience for most people, and these questions and answers can help with the educational component of IPT, especially during the initial phases. Many of the questions will be useful particularly to the novice therapist and patients.

Therapeutic Issues

Personality

A frequent issue clinicians face is whether to focus on Axis I or Axis II: Is the problem a psychiatric illness or a personality disorder? Syndromes on the two axes can coexist, but it is not always clear when to attribute symptoms to one axis or the other. A personality disorder may lead to dysfunctional behavior that yields poor outcomes in life and increases the risk of developing a depressive episode. Conversely, an episode of major depression or dysthymic disorder may heighten or mimic personality traits, creating the clinical impression of a personality disorder that may then remit if the mood disorder does (Markowitz, 1998).

IPT does not focus on the patient's personality, nor does it generally expect to change it. The one exception to date is the effort to modify IPT to treat borderline personality disorder (BPD) (see Chapter 21). The focus on Axis I does not mean that personality can be ignored. The presence of a personality disorder may be illusory or may complicate treatment, but it should not dissuade you from IPT treatment.

The IPT stance on personality comprises the following:

- Patients who become depressed and who have other psychiatric disorders do not have unique personality traits.

- Symptoms of an Axis I disorder can mimic an Axis II diagnosis, and any definitive personality assessment should await resolution of the acute symptom state. For example, a major depressive episode may create the impression of a personality disorder that then remits if the mood disorder does (Markowitz, 1998). Depression instills social anxiety, passivity (which may sometimes be misinterpreted as passive aggression), and avoidance of confrontation, which can easily be confused with Axis II Cluster C personality disorders. It can be almost impossible to accurately distinguish an illness state from a personality trait in the presence of an Axis I disorder. Treating the Axis I disorder may clarify whether an Axis II disorder actually existed or just appeared to do so.
- A patient can have an Axis I and II disorder concurrently. With short-term psychotherapy, the outcome in such patients is expected to be less favorable than in those with mild or no personality pathology, just as Axis I or Axis III comorbidity may complicate treatment. Nonetheless, IPT may be used for acute symptom remission in the face of comorbid diagnoses.
- Personality problems may complicate treatment, altering the patient-therapist relationship and making it more difficult to manage (Foley, O'Malley, Rounsaville, Prusoff, & Weissman, 1987). Focusing on current interpersonal problems may be helpful even if the problems are largely due to the patient's behavior (as opposed to that of a significant other).

A patient with a paranoid stance, for example, needs to be approached with an understanding of the implications of that perspective. The therapist may anticipate suspiciousness, disarm it with openness, and avoid threatening the patient by either acting too distant (and uninterested) or becoming too intimate (and hence threatening). A dependent patient is likely to defer to therapeutic authority, a behavior that may be linked to depression; with such patients, the therapist should be careful to encourage capability and independence rather than to accept an authoritarian role. On the other hand, such patients may respond well to psychoeducation and clinical injunctions from the therapist ("*If you are feeling more suicidal, you must go to an emergency room!*"). A general clinical knowledge of personality disorders may be helpful in guiding the therapist's response to such characterological behaviors, whether these are artifacts of depression or not. The IPT therapist attributes symptoms—including seeming character traits—to the depressive illness and does *not* blame the person's character (Markowitz, 1998). That is, the typical IPT use of the sick role (see Chapter 2) to excuse the patient for symptoms continues to apply. The therapist can say:

> *You keep blaming yourself for these behaviors, but I see them as part of your depression. People who are depressed see themselves as defective, but*

that's a part of the illness. Once we treat your depression and you're feeling better, we'll see what your "character" is like.

Personality may be a determinant of the patient's recurrent interpersonal problems. Although IPT therapists may not attempt to explore antecedents of personality functioning or to change personality, they may help patients to recognize maladaptive personality features. For instance, to a patient with mild paranoid tendencies, the therapist may point out a disposition to be touchy with certain people under certain conditions and then explore the interpersonal consequences. Personality has so far not been found to be an important determinant of short-term outcome in IPT (Zuckerman, Prusoff, Weissman, & Padian, 1980).

In the NIMH Treatment of Depression Collaborative Research Program, one analysis of patients who *completed* the study found that depressed patients with obsessive traits responded better to IPT than to cognitive behavioral therapy (CBT), whereas patients with avoidant traits (i.e., those isolated patients in the interpersonal deficits category) did better with CBT than IPT (Barber and Muenz, 1996). This finding did not apply to the treatment sample as a whole, however. In a study of depressed HIV-positive patients, the majority of whom met criteria for an Axis II personality disorder at the time of study entry, the presence of a personality disorder was associated with a slightly higher Hamilton Rating Scale for Depression score at both baseline and end-point compared to depressed patients without personality disorders. Yet the improvement in depressive symptoms was equal during the 16-week trial (Markowitz, Svartberg, & Swartz, 1998). These findings support the use of IPT for depressed patients with or without apparent personality disorders:

- Although IPT does not target personality disorder (except for borderline personality disorder) as a treatment, it has been shown to build social skills. Without fundamentally altering personality structure, IPT can thus significantly improve overall functioning even in the presence of a personality disorder. Learning to be more assertive in disputes or to manage anger and to develop alternative ways of handling relationships may be just as useful as directly treating the personality disorder.
- By relieving depressive symptoms, IPT may improve maladaptive personality traits (Cyranowski et al., 2004; Shea et al., 2002).

Mobilizing the Passive Patient

Patients when depressed tend to be passive, unassertive, and socially withdrawn. They fear the kinds of confrontations that are necessary to many aspects of social interaction, particularly asserting their own needs and wishes, setting limits, and expressing anger. Therapists sometimes get patients to agree that they should be angry in a particular situation, but they are then reluctant to express it, fearing that anger is a bad emotion, that it will destroy the relationship, and so on. A common clinical dilemma, then, is how to mobilize patients to take needed action.

One approach is to use the concept of a *transgression*. When a significant other breaks a written or an unwritten social code, such as physically hurting the patient, having an affair, or behaving sadistically, the therapist may label this a transgression—the kind of behavior that everyone in society would agree is unacceptable. This arms the patient with the right to an apology, at the very least. This conceptualization of interpersonal transgressions provides a helpful framework for some patients in thinking they have a moral right to redress.

Dealing with the transgression can then be explored in the usual IPT manner:

1. exploring the patient's feelings (e.g., anger, sense of betrayal, disgust) about having been mistreated, which the therapist can then validate
2. investigating interpersonal options for expressing these feelings
3. having chosen an option, role-playing the encounter so that patients can say what they want to say and in a tone of voice appropriate to the context

Patients in role disputes who follow this route to seeking an apology or other redress often feel liberated and vindicated by the experience.

The Intellectualizing Patient

Some patients avoid dealing with frightening affects by keeping therapy on an abstract, intellectualized plane. They may do unassigned background reading about psychotherapy, employ psychotherapeutic jargon, and speak in generalities. None of this is conducive to effective psychotherapy.

It is important to keep IPT grounded in affect. Therapy feels meaningful when it teems with feeling related to important issues in the patient's life. The structure of IPT sessions facilitates this approach by focusing each meeting on a recent, affectively charged event in the patient's life. *("How have things been since we last met? . . . I'm sorry to hear that; was there something that happened in the past week that contributed to your feeling so bad?")* The IPT therapist should focus on specific events and the patient's reactions to them as a way of keeping the therapy affectively alive. One guide to the emotional vitality of the session is therapeutic boredom, which may indicate that the treatment is becoming affectless. If the patient becomes vague or discursive, the therapist can ask, *"For example?"* and then elicit the patient's emotional responses to that example.

When emotion wells up during a session, linger and savor it. As a therapist, you want the patient to come to understand that strong emotions need not be avoided. Such shared emotional epiphanies are likely to stay with the patient and to add impact to the therapeutic process. Do not intervene until the patient has had some time to recognize, live with, and develop some comfort with and control over the feeling. Patients should learn in IPT that feelings, depressive and otherwise, are powerful but at the same time are only feelings. In IPT, patients should recognize that they can use these emotions to understand interpersonal events. They should grasp that they can come to express themselves effectively and develop some control over their feelings.

Keeping to the Focus

Holding the patient to the agreed-upon focus can be a challenge. Particularly at the start of treatment, patients may not know what to expect and may digress to a variety of topics. Once you have determined the focal problem area, described it to the patient in a formulation, and obtained the patient's agreement to work on this focus, you can and should invoke it as the therapy progresses. Bringing up the focus reminds the patient of the central theme of the depressive episode and provides a sense of thematic continuity to the therapy.

If you have chosen the interpersonal problem area well, the incident elicited at the start of most sessions *("How have things been since we last met?")* will fit within the treatment framework. For example, sadness and loneliness during the week may be tied to complicated bereavement, or marital strife may be connected with a role dispute. Sometimes the patient will raise an interpersonal situation that resonates with the current theme (e.g., a parallel to a marital role dispute). If so, help the patient solve it, then point out the parallel. With your encouragement, the patient will soon learn to stay on track until the problem area is resolved.

Short digressions can be tolerated, but you do not want the treatment to meander so far as to lose its direction and shape. If the patient deviates, listen carefully—you do not want to disparage information that the patient feels is important—but try to resolve the extraneous issue quickly and remind the patient of the focus you had both decided would be central to the treatment. Returning to the focus should not be a mechanical and artificial process but rather an organizing motif for the treatment. If the problem area clearly needs to shift because of new material brought up, this move should be made explicit.

Sticking to the Time Limit

Psychotherapists who are not used to time limits may need practice to adjust to the pressure induced by a 12-week cutoff point. Such a constraint indeed pressures both therapist and patient to work hard and quickly. Hence the therapist should resist the temptation to dilute this pressure by failing to fully define the treatment length or granting extra sessions without an imperative rationale. "We'll work for 12 to 16 sessions" is unnecessarily vague; make the limit precisely 12, 14, or 16. The exact number is less meaningful than that there be an exact number.

Sessions should be weekly, allowing time between sessions for things to happen in the patient's life yet maintaining momentum. Plan for vacations at the start of treatment. Try to make up sessions if you or the patient has to cancel one (therapist flexibility is a virtue patients appreciate), while keeping to the overall threshold. If you take the time limit seriously, so will the patient.

If a patient comes late to sessions, attribute this lateness to the patient's depressive illness rather than personality pathology. Such an attribution fits the IPT medical model, facilitates the therapeutic alliance, and is likely to be accurate for depressed patients. If you have the time to tag on a few minutes at the end of a late-starting session, it is worth doing so.

Silence

Silence occurs in any therapy and is a normal part of the treatment. It may indicate the patient's discomfort with treatment and avoidance of emotionally charged material. IPT is a treatment in which the patient and the therapist share responsibility for bringing up topics to discuss and explore. When emotionally laden material has been discussed, a period of silence may follow. If a situation is very charged, there may be a few moments during which the patients cannot talk about it. The therapist will probably not probe because it might be more helpful to wait for the material to come up spontaneously. You might explain to the patient:

> *Silence does not necessarily mean that no work is going on. The therapy involves sharing the experiences of the time, which may include silence as well as active discussion.*

If silence becomes a persistent problem, it will require a discussion. You might say:

> *It's possible that you have done so well and are feeling so good that there is nothing more to talk about. In this case, we should talk about terminating treatment. . . . If you don't feel that the problems are solved, then you might try to figure out what is making it hard to discuss how you're feeling. Are you feeling guilty about something? Ashamed? Fearful of what I might think about what's on your mind? Do you feel that something is inappropriate? That I'll disapprove?*

Some patients use silence as an interpersonal style: They pout or sulk rather than voicing legitimate complaints. If this is the case with your patient, you may address the issue directly without framing it as a criticism:

> *When you're feeling depressed, is it hard to let someone know when you're feeling upset with him? . . . If this is the case, it might be helpful to look at*

the effects your silence has on others and whether it is an effective form of communication for you.

The therapist may also make the point that:

There are no "bad" feelings in this therapy. Your feelings tell us something about what's going on in your life, and they can be helpful guideposts to understanding your situation. Even if it feels awkward, I would encourage you to let me know as much as you can about how you're feeling.

Technical Issues

Many therapists may view psychotherapy purely as two people talking in a room. As such, rating scales and recording devices may seem uncomfortable intrusions at first. Yet both are important aspects of IPT.

Choose a rating instrument for depression (or the appropriate target syndrome) and get to know it. The American Psychiatric Association's *Handbook of Psychiatric Measures* (2000) lists a variety of scales that either you (e.g., the Hamilton Rating Scale for Depression) or the patient (e.g., the Beck Depression Inventory) can complete to assess symptom severity. Get used to administering the scale both at intake and at regular intervals during the treatment. You will find that measuring symptoms in this way keeps both you and the patient attuned to progress. As symptoms diminish, you can congratulate patients on their progress:

"You've cut your score in half already!" "Your Hamilton Depression score is now 7—a big improvement from the 22 you started with. You are officially in clinical remission! Good work!"

Many clinicians who get into the habit of using rating scales in IPT subsequently use them in all of their treatments.

You may also want to record your treatment sessions for supervisory purposes. An actual tape of the session is the best way to evaluate the therapeutic process because it is far more accurate and less intrusive than process notes. Like a therapist in an IPT session, your supervisor will want to know what each of you said and how it felt. If you do record sessions, you should obtain the patient's written consent for taping and explain the purpose of doing so, your concern for protecting the patient's confidentiality, and what will happen to the tapes:

I will be using this only for supervisory purposes; only my supervisor, an IPT expert, will be listening to the tape, which I will keep in a locked drawer and erase at the end of the treatment.

Therapists tend to be more worried about the taping process than patients are. You may at first feel self-conscious with a tape or video recorder running, but you are likely to learn a lot from the experience and to adjust to the process after a few sessions. Later you may be pleased to have recorded your finest therapeutic moments on tape—rather than your worst, as you may initially fear!

Comparison With Other Treatments

Hundreds of forms of psychotherapy have been cited in the literature of the past century. Most of these represent the personal approaches of charismatic psychotherapists, and the overwhelming majority have never been tested for efficacy. IPT inevitably overlaps with some of these approaches in using particular techniques. It is the coherence of its interpersonal strategies and its targeting of psychiatric disorders as medical illnesses, rather than the particular techniques involved, that define IPT as a treatment. Nonetheless, there are some techniques that IPT does not use.

The two psychotherapies to which IPT is most often compared are psychodynamic psychotherapy and cognitive behavioral therapy. Many IPT therapists have undergone training in one or the other of these backgrounds. Compared to psychodynamic psychotherapy, IPT focuses more on the here and now, rather than on childhood antecedents; it focuses on the patient's life outside the office rather than on the therapeutic relationship within it; and it does not interpret dreams or transference. IPT takes a more organized, outcome-focused approach to changing interpersonal patterns as a method of relieving symptoms of a depressive or other psychiatric syndrome (Markowitz et al., 1998).

Like IPT, CBT is an often time-limited treatment that has been applied to a range of psychiatric diagnoses. Whereas IPT focuses on affect and behavior in interpersonal relationships, CBT focuses on the irrational thoughts (cognitions) that arise in such contexts. If IPT is more structured than psychodynamic psychotherapy, CBT is still more structured than IPT, frequently beginning each session by developing an agenda for the meeting. CBT therapists assign homework, including undertaking specific activities and making lists of cognitions. In contrast, IPT assigns no homework unless the resolution of the interpersonal problem areas (e.g., role dispute) within the framework of the treatment time limit is considered a kind of grand therapeutic assignment. As this description illustrates, IPT differs from both psychodynamic psychotherapy and CBT, eschewing many of their key techniques.

IPT has been called a "supportive psychotherapy." This often amorphous and originally pejorative term once referred to psychodynamic psychotherapy for patients too ill to tolerate transferential interpretations. Since IPT does not involve interpretations, it is in that sense a supportive psychotherapy. More modern definitions of supportive psychotherapy (e.g., Novalis, Rojcewicz, & Peele, 1993; Pinsker, 1997) emphasize the so-called common factors of psychotherapy (J. Frank, 1971): release of affect, helping the patient feel understood, building a strong therapeutic alliance, and so on. In this sense, IPT contains elements of supportive psychotherapy but also includes specific interpersonal interventions and strategies that many supportive therapists would use far less often and less systematically. None of the other psychotherapies explicitly focus on the problem areas.

Patient Questions

How Does IPT Work?

Most patients, especially if they have never been in psychotherapy, have legitimate questions about how talking to a stranger can help them with their problems. The patient can be told:

> *The elements of psychotherapy are not a mystery. Psychotherapy involves a relationship with someone you can trust, who will be an advocate for you, who will hold what you say in strict confidence, and who will not take a judgmental approach or decide what is right or wrong for you. In interpersonal psychotherapy we work on the connection between your feelings and your life situation. In the next X weeks, I will try to help you to work on unfulfilled wishes and problematic relationships that are contributing to your depression. You should begin to become more comfortable with your feelings in problematic close relationships and decide how to use them to change the relationship/situation.*

What Credentials Should My Therapist Have?

IPT is designed for use by psychiatrists, psychologists, primary care physicians, psychiatric social workers, psychiatric nurses, and other health professional who have had at least several years of clinical experience in psychotherapy with depressed patients.

Patients who ask should be informed about the therapist's credentials. Usually, questions about credentials reflect discomfort with the therapeutic situation. In the beginning most patients without prior treatment experience do not feel comfortable since the therapeutic situation feels unnatural. Encourage patients to discuss their discomfort directly and determine with you whether the problem is not just discomfort in seeking help. The patient should be reassured that, beyond the therapist's credentials, the patient needs to feel comfortable with the therapist. The option of finding another therapist should always be available. Make it clear that you will not be insulted if the patient wants to consider a different treatment or therapist. At the same time, it is important not to present such nonchalance in offering an alternative referral that the patient finds you uncaring or rejecting.

I Thought It Didn't Matter If I Came Late

Patients new to psychotherapy who are used to attending crowded clinics with long waits, where appointment times are relatively meaningless, may not show up on time. In such cases the therapist needs to help the patient acculturate to psychotherapy. This means explaining that the sessions need to begin and end on time and that this time has been set aside for the patient. The time limit of IPT can be used to emphasize the importance of the therapy session. For example, *"We have only nine sessions left."* Sometimes patients may arrive late because of practical problems such as transportation or baby-sitters. This should be discussed. However, it is also useful to relate the lateness to the patients' feeling of hopelessness about their condition and the value of treatment and also the fact that being depressed may make it difficult for them to get to sessions. You can offer a supportive statement such as: *"It is hard to get to treatment when you are feeling so bad and when you haven't slept and don't have much energy."*

This avoids blaming the patient for the depressive symptoms that may underlie not coming to treatment. Of course the patient's attendance may waver with the discussion of sessions on topics that are anxiety provoking and stressful. The patient may also feel that treatment is not helping or that life perhaps is getting better and thus not want to spend the time in discussions. It is useful to talk about these issues directly.

Can My Family Come to the Treatment?

IPT was designed as an individual treatment and generally stays that way. Most IPT therapists have been individual psychotherapists, with less expertise in couples or family treatment. Depressed patients may ask about involving family members because they feel inadequate to the task of therapy themselves. Yet their prognosis is good, and if they do participate in IPT, they can leave with full credit for their gains.

Nonetheless, it is sometimes helpful to have significant family members (spouse, parents) participate in one or more therapy sessions if there are marital or parent/child problems and if both the patient and the significant other are willing to do so. These joint sessions that may be used to acquire additional information, obtain the cooperation of the significant other, or facilitate some interpersonal problem solving and communication. For couples who have marital disputes, a conjoint marital IPT has been developed for use when both parties want to participate (see Chapter 23). The patient should feel free to ask the therapist whether a family member can attend, and the therapist may also request the person's attendance, especially in the initial sessions. In treating minors, parents should be involved to provide consent and often attend the initial sessions (see Chapter 13).

The participation of a family member, however, must not violate confidentiality. The therapist must clarify ahead of time what will and will not be discussed in conjoint sessions: that you will not discuss the content of the patient sessions with the other person and that any additional contact the other person has with the therapist will be reported and discussed with the patient.

Do I Need a Different Treatment?

No treatment benefits all patients. In some cases, patients do need different treatment while in IPT, including referral to another kind of psychotherapy (e.g., CBT) or for psychotropic medication (the latter with or without IPT). These options should be openly discussed at the beginning of therapy so that the patient feels permitted to inquire about alternatives during the course of therapy. An additional consultation with a psychiatrist may be useful for patients not in therapy with a psychiatrist. This exploration of therapeutic options is consonant with the IPT medical model and with the pragmatic IPT emphasis on the exploration of options.

On the other hand, some depressed patients ask the question because they are skeptical about *all* treatment. They may be reassured that their chances of improving are good even if they won't fully believe that until they're better. If a patient has not had at least a 50% reduction in symptoms or a complete remission at the end of 12 sessions or 12 weeks, a different psychotherapy or the addition of medication (or switch of medication) should be considered.

Will I Get Along on My Own at the End of the Treatment?

Patients are more apt to have this concern during time-limited psychotherapy. Yet depressed patients (and sometimes their therapists) often underestimate their capabilities. The patient may expect to have difficulty functioning without the therapist's guidance, especially if it has been useful. The patient can be told that the dependency on the therapist is focused and limited. The therapist will help patients recognize their own personal strengths and capabilities. As they begin to feel better and to deal better with interpersonal problems, some of the reliance on their therapist will disappear. However, the option for additional (or different) therapy is always there at the end of a course of treatment.

What If I Want to End Treatment Early?

The patient may wish to terminate early because the patient and therapist disagree about the therapy contract; the patient feels the continuation of therapy is threatening; or the patient believes the problem has been satisfactorily dealt with. A frank discussion here is quite useful. Ask questions such as the following:

- *If you want to end the treatment early, we should consider why you do.*
- *Are you no longer depressed?*
- *Are these issues too painful or frightening to confront?*

- *Is there some problem between the two of us that we haven't discussed?*
- *Do you feel that IPT is not the right treatment for you, in which case alternatives should be considered?*

The therapist should indicate that the main goal is to help the patient feel better and not to tie that person to the treatment.

Is My Depression Biological?

As information about the biological basis of depression reaches the popular press, patients increasingly ask questions about a cause: "Is my depression due to a chemical imbalance or my stressful marriage?" Debates about whether depressions are biological or psychological miss the point. The patient might be told:

> *All depressions have a biological component. They are associated with changes in sleep, appetite, energy levels, and concentration. The feelings of depression reflect brain chemistry. These biological changes, as well as the increasing information about genetic vulnerability to depression, do not change the fact that all depressions also occur in a psychosocial context. A person's mood can be markedly altered by upsetting changes in relationships with others—in your case, by the marital dispute you've been talking about. Research has shown that stressful life events can trigger episodes of depression in genetically vulnerable people.*
>
> *We can't do much to change genes, and the precise genetic vulnerability is still unclear, but much can be done in psychotherapy to identify and handle the stressful life situation. Depression usually responds to medication or psychotherapy or a combination of the two. Biology and psychosocial context are intimately related and difficult to separate from each other. That may explain why both psychotherapy and medication work on symptoms that appear very biological (e.g., loss of appetite), as well as those that appear more psychological (e.g., feelings of guilt, low self-esteem). Neuroimaging studies have shown that psychotherapy changes your brain chemistry: It's a biological treatment.*

(References for IPT neuroimaging studies are taken from Brody et al., 2001; Martin, Martin, Rai, Richardson, & Royall, 2001.)

Can I Give Depression to My Children?

There is little question that depression is a family affair. The children of depressed parents carry a two to three times greater risk for becoming depressed than the children of parents who have never been depressed. Put another way, if the average rate of depression is 3%, the risk for children of depressed parents is 6–9%. The good news is that most of the children will not get depressed. We do not know the mechanisms by which depression is transmitted in families, whether it is through genes, learning, stress, or some combination. The patient can be told:

> *If you are depressed and your children seem to be having similar problems, pay attention, take it seriously, talk to them about it, and get them help. There is good evidence that the improvement of your symptoms will have a positive effect on your children. Relief from stressful events and better handling of them, possibly through psychotherapy, may help to reduce or eliminate the triggers of depression both in you and in your vulnerable family members.*

Consonant with the IPT model, it is also important to emphasize that the depressive risk to children, like the patient's depression itself, is not the patient's fault: Depression is a medical illness, comparable to high blood pressure or arthritis, that tends to run in families. We can also now tell the patient that there is evidence that their remission will have a beneficial effect on their children's symptoms (Weissman, Pilowsky, et al., 2006).

What About Alcohol and Drugs?

There is a high comorbidity between depression and alcohol abuse, particularly in depressed men. Depressed patients may try in various ways to relieve their symptoms before coming for treatment, and alcohol is an enticing solution. In the short run, alcohol can relieve anxiety, improve mood, help the depressed individual sleep, and dull painful memories and anxiety. The patient should be told:

> *Alcohol feels good in the short run, but it's a bad treatment for depression and in the long run. While it can help your mood and sleep at first, over time it disturbs sleep and is a mood depressant. It can diminish your ability to cope, it creates additional problems with family and at work, it interferes with treatment, and it may increase one's risk of suicide. There's also the risk of ending up with two problems, depression and alcoholism.*

Part of taking a good initial history involves asking about drug and alcohol use (see Chapter 2). Ask patients about their use of alcohol, recreational drugs, and prescription medications. If patients are also taking antidepressant or other medications, these may compound the effects of alcohol. Patients with heavy or chronic substance use may require detoxification prior to or concomitant with antidepressant treatment. Your goal as an IPT therapist is to help the patient substitute healthy interpersonal responses, using improved communication to reach outward, for the tendency to reach for the bottle and retreat inward.

Is My Depression Incurable?

Patients with acute depressive symptoms feel hopeless. You can tell them:

When you are acutely depressed, it is common to feel that the symptoms will last forever. However, with proper treatment, more than half of the time depression responds; about 50% of patients will have a remission of symptoms in 4–6 weeks. As your sleep and appetite problems begin to resolve, you will find that your mood improves. There are many different types of effective treatments for depression. IPT is just one of them. I can't promise you that IPT will help you, but there is a very good chance it will. And if it doesn't, there are other types of psychotherapies and a range of medications that can help. So if one treatment does not work, there are plenty of alternatives to try. Give the treatment time to work. Don't let the hopelessness of depression discourage you from continuing: That hopelessness is a very misleading symptom since your prognosis is in fact good.

What If I Have Thoughts of Suicide?

Most depressed patients are suffering and feel hopeless about the future, so the thought of suicide is a common one. Suicide is the greatest risk depression brings. Inquiries about suicidal thoughts, plans, and attempts should be part of the initial evaluation and pursued directly during treatment as needed:

The symptoms of depression can be overwhelming and invade every part of your life. You feel your life is out of control. Suicidal thoughts are symptoms of depression. You may feel life is not worth living, wish you were dead, or perhaps think about killing yourself. If you feel this way, please let me know! If the feelings get stronger, we can have more frequent contacts either in person or by phone.

And don't do it! Suicide is the greatest risk of depression. You have to stay alive long enough to get better: As the depression improves, you're likely to again feel that life is worth living. People who are no longer depressed don't want to kill themselves, and you have in fact a great chance of getting better in treatment.

Will Depression Reoccur When IPT Ends?

Most patients who recover from a depressive episode are concerned about whether they will have a relapse or a recurrence. This is especially true in a treatment that is time limited. About 30–40% of people who have a depressive episode will never have another one (Judd et al., 1998). Yet over a lifetime, most patients have recurrences, usually in the face of a life event. Patient education during IPT can help them to understand and anticipate situations that could provoke recurrence and either find ways to handle them or seek early treatment. Our information on the prevention of recurrences is increasing, and the patient might be told that vulnerability to depression is the same kind of medical vulnerability that puts people at risk for high blood pressure, asthma, high cholesterol, or heart disease. You can say:

We will talk about situations that might put you at risk for another episode, and hopefully you will be able to deal with those situations before they get to you and result in symptoms. You should also leave here expert in recognizing early symptoms of depression. (That's one reason we keep doing the Hamilton Rating Scale for Depression.) If you should get depressed in the future, the important thing to remember is that it's a treatable illness, it's not your fault, and you just need to return for treatment, the way you would for any other medical problem.

Patients who have had multiple episodes of major depression are at high risk for further episodes. IPT has shown efficacy as a maintenance treatment for depression (see Chapter 11). Thus, ongoing IPT is an option for patients who have benefited from acute IPT but remain at high risk for relapse or recurrence.

Section II

*Adaptations of IPT
for Mood Disorders*

10

Overview of Adaptations of IPT

The success of IPT as a treatment for acute major depressive episodes has led to its adaptation and testing for patients diagnosed with other mood and non–mood disorders and in different formats. All of these modified treatments follow the general IPT principles already described. Some have been detailed in separate manuals, which contain usually minor changes, relevant to the specific disorder, age group, or treatment format they address (see reference list of manuals). Here we summarize these adaptations. Some issues to consider are time (duration of treatment), experience, and empirical support. We recommend that the clinician review the *DSM-IV* diagnostic criteria for the particular modification of interest (American Psychiatric Association, 1994).

Time

Studies of IPT for acute major depressive disorder have used a preset time limit of 12 or 16 sessions in as many weeks. This time, or "dosage," interval has been altered for some of the adaptations that follow. As is true for most psychotherapies, the optimal number of sessions in IPT has received relatively little testing. In clinical practice, some flexibility may be reasonable to adjust for vacations, upsetting events occurring late in therapy, and so on. Yet it is important in IPT to set and hold to a time limit of some kind. The pressure of time helps propel the therapy forward.

Experience

This book will not equip you as a clinician to treat all patients with all diagnoses or to use IPT in a group format if you have never done group therapy. To effectively treat patients who carry a particular diagnosis, you must not only learn IPT but also have experience in working with patients to whom that adaptation applies. To treat depressed adolescents, patients with eating disorders, or those with borderline personality disorder, the clinician should know the clinical terrain, as well as the psychotherapeutic approach. In the same way, in order to work with patients in conjoint (couples) or group IPT, you should have familiarity with those treatment modalities.

Empirical Support

The level of empirical support for each of these adaptations varies and will shift as new studies are conducted. In order to guide the reader, we have developed the following shorthand scale to rate the strength of empirical foundation for each of the adaptations that follows:

> **** (4 stars): Treatment has been validated by at least two randomized controlled trials demonstrating the superiority of IPT to a control condition. This generally qualifies treatments for inclusion in treatment guidelines, such as is the case for IPT for major depressive disorder.

> *** (3 stars): Validation by at least one randomized controlled trial or equivalent to a reference treatment of established efficacy

> ** (2 stars): Encouraging findings in one or more open trials or in pilot studies with small samples (< 12 subjects)

> * (1 star): Undergoing testing or not tested

> (No stars): Negative findings (IPT has been found to be no better than a control condition)

11

Maintenance Treatment of Depression

IPT was designed as an acute, time-limited treatment. Resolving an episode of major depression using IPT takes 12–16 weeks. It would be nice if the problem ended there, but unfortunately it often does not. Even patients who have remitted from a first episode of major depression face the likelihood of a relapse or recurrence at some point. Patients who have had multiple episodes are almost sure to have more unless given antidepressant prophylaxis (Judd et al., 1998; Judd and Akiskal, 2000).

The termination phase at the end of a successful course of IPT treatment should include discussion of the possibility that depression could recur and that if it does, it is not the patient's fault but the return of a potentially recurrent illness. Under such circumstances the patient should seek further treatment. If the patient has had a single episode of depression and has few residual symptoms, it may be appropriate to send the patient home with this advice. Although the patient is likely to experience another episode at some point in life, it may never happen or not occur for many years.

If the patient has had multiple prior depressive episodes or has improved in IPT but still reports a high level of residual symptoms, then the patient is at high risk of relapse, and prophylactic interventions should be discussed as part of the termination. Medication has been the most carefully studied intervention and has yielded the most consistently efficacious prophylaxis of relapse of major depression. However, cognitive behavioral therapy (CBT) and IPT have also shown preventive benefits for patients. Thus, maintenance IPT should be considered as an option for continued treatment.

In addition to those with recurrent depression, patients who should be considered for maintenance IPT include women during pregnancy and lactation, for whom medication may not be possible or optimal but who can be maintained with a lower probability of relapse if they receive IPT. Elderly depressed patients who may not tolerate medication, as well as patients who have a history of recurrence but do not wish to take medication, are candidates for maintenance treatment. The evidence for the efficacy of IPT weekly for 6 months as a continuation treatment (or monthly for 3 years of maintenance treatment) is quite strong.

Repeated research trials have demonstrated not only that IPT can help patients to remit from major depression but also that maintenance IPT (IPT-M), even at the low dose of one monthly session, can preserve euthymia for patients and forestall the return of depressive symptoms even for patients at very high risk for relapse (Frank et al., 1990; Frank, Kupfer, Wagner, McEachran, & Cornes, 1991; Reynolds, III, Frank, Dew, et al., 1999; Reynolds, III, Frank, Perel, et al., 1999).

Level of Evidence: **** Treatment has been validated by at least two randomized controlled trials demonstrating the superiority of IPT to a control condition. (The exception is a study showing that monthly maintenance IPT was not as efficacious as medication for depressed patients who were older than 70 years of age [Reynolds, III, et al., 2006].)

Adaptation

Maintenance IPT is in most respects like IPT as acute treatment. The focus remains on interpersonal functioning and mood in relation to life events.

1. *Time limit and frequency.* Although IPT-M may be a chronic treatment, it is still arranged as a time-limited contract between therapist and patient. IPT-M has been tested mainly as a weekly treatment for 6 months (Klerman, DiMascio, Weissman, Prusoff, & Paykel, 1974) or as a monthly treatment for 3 years. Its frequency can be varied in clinical practice depending upon what patient and therapist deem appropriate and desirable. Maintenance IPT could conceivably continue the weekly schedule of acute IPT, or sessions might take place every 2, 3, or 4 weeks for a specified number of years. At the end of that period, therapist and patient should again discuss a renegotiation of the therapy.

2. *Focus.* Unlike acute IPT, maintenance treatment begins when the patient is not acutely ill. The goals of maintenance treatment are to minimize residual symptoms and to ward off the return of others rather than to reduce the symptoms of an acute episode. The sessions may include review of the emergence of symptoms or the appearance of problems that had been associated with their onset. Since patient and therapist will have worked together in the acute treatment, the themes of the acute treatment usually continue. It may be possible to complete work on role disputes, role transitions, and so on that began during the acute phase.

    If maintenance treatment continues for several years, it is also possible that new events will occur and new interpersonal foci will arise. A patient who has previously worked on a role dispute may suffer bereavement when a loved one dies. Hence one aspect of IPT-M is the flexibility to shift foci as circumstances dictate. Regardless of the focus, the general themes remain the same:

- Depression is a treatable illness that is not the patient's fault.
- Interpersonal situations influence mood, and vice versa.
- IPT works to help the patient to recognize the connection between emotions and life circumstances and to develop skills to express those feelings in interpersonal circumstances in order to make life go better.

3. *Consolidation.* Patients who have responded well to antidepressant treatments often feel better but experience their euthymia as fragile (Markowitz, 1993). It may take weeks or months for self-confidence to really take hold in the aftermath of a depressive episode that had left the patient feeling helpless, hopeless, and worthless. New social skills may require additional practice to feel comfortable, as is reflected in research that shows that these skills grow during the year following acute treatment (Weissman, Klerman, Prusoff, Sholomskas, & Padian, 1981) and that seeming personality traits recede over time in IPT-M (Cyranowski et al., 2004). Hence maintenance treatment is a time to further initial growth in therapy and to encourage patients to test their abilities and take appropriate risks in social circumstances.

4. *Techniques:* IPT-M uses the same techniques described in Chapter 8.

Case Example: Speaking Up Takes Time

Roger, a 34-year-old single male violinist in a prominent orchestra, presented with his third episode of major depression, which followed a panic attack at an important audition. He had hoped this audition would move him to the highest rung in his profession, but he had blanked, frozen, and forgotten his piece, then retreated in shame and horror to his room for two weeks. He presented with depressed and anxious mood; sleep and appetite disturbance; social withdrawal; extreme self-criticism; feelings of helplessness, hopelessness, worthlessness; and passive suicidal ideation. His Ham-D score was 28, and he met criteria for recurrent major depressive disorder, social anxiety disorder, and avoidant personality disorder. "My music is my life," he said, and he had been too depressed to play in the past month.

Roger was a chronically shy, socially isolated man whose closest relationship had always been with his single, artistically pretentious, domineering stage mother, whom he lived with. He both resented her control of his life and depended on her. She had interfered in the few romantic relationships he had dared to attempt. His two previous depressive episodes had occurred following his graduation from the conservatory at age 21 and after his mother's humiliation of him in front of a would-be fiancée when he was 25. Each episode had responded to a course of medication.

A 12-week course of IPT focused on the *role transition* in his career. With the therapist's encouragement, Roger prepared for and sought another audition, in which he played well and won a desired audition. He and his therapist discussed his problematic relationships, which included a fear of criticism by his famous and famously stringent conductor, social discomfort in dealing with his colleagues, and deferential ambivalence toward his mother. He increased his hobbies during acute treatment but formed few new relationships. Nonetheless, his Ham-D score fell to 8.

Because of Roger's history of recurrent depression, his therapist congratulated him on his gains in acute treatment but suggested that he was at risk for recurrence and might benefit from maintenance IPT to avoid a future depressive episode. They contracted for 2 more years of monthly treatment, with the idea that he could use the additional therapy not only to further his career but also to work more on interpersonal relationships. The first issue they dealt with was his social discomfort in professional situations. Roger remained insecure about his status in the orchestra because he believed that the conductor did not really like him. Roger and his therapist discussed this anxiety as a symptom of depression and social anxiety. After considerable role-playing over several months, he made an appointment to speak to the eminent and imperious maestro. To his surprise, when Roger expressed his worries about his performance, the great man responded kindly and supportively. This successful experience enabled Roger to relax somewhat with his fellow musicians and even to go out with them for drinks on occasion. This activity, however, aroused his mother's ire.

In the second year of maintenance, Roger remained euthymic and less anxious. He felt more comfortable at work, but now, at age 35, he wanted to develop a romantic relationship, which meant setting limits with his mother. He had met Jeannie, a flautist he liked, but was afraid to bring her home to Mom. Treatment shifted to a focus on the smoldering *role dispute* between Roger and his mother. This was an unsettling time for Roger, who asked for more frequent, fortnightly sessions for the subsequent 6 weeks. The therapist agreed.

In these sessions Roger expressed his anger about crossing his mother and his fear that she might either abandon him or have a heart attack and die if he disappointed her. He had attempted few arguments with her and had never won one. The therapist validated Roger's anger at his mother's selfishly oppressive behavior. They explored his options for discussing the situation with her: He had never discussed relationships with her directly. "Mom, it's time I had a girlfriend, and you shouldn't interfere. It doesn't mean I don't love you," he decided to say. He hesitated to confront her but finally did. His mother had a fit, but this had been anticipated in therapy, and Roger was able to stand his ground. His mother finally backed off, and he continued his relationship with Jeannie and finally brought her home to meet his mother.

He had survived. Roger remained euthymic after 2 years of IPT-M; his Ham-D score had hovered under 5 in the final 6 months. He recontracted for an additional 2 years of bimonthly IPT-M, during which he got engaged, married, and moved out of his mother's apartment. He had developed some friendships and was prospering in his career. He no longer met criteria for either major depression or anxiety disorder.

12

Pregnancy, Miscarriage, and Postpartum Depression

Overview

The idea of pregnancy as a time of unconditional well-being is a myth. Ten percent of pregnant women experience major depression, and, for many of them, the depression continues into the postpartum period. Complications of pregnancy and miscarriage can lead to chronic depression. New baby blues (i.e., mild depressive symptoms in the 6 months following childbirth) are so common as to be considered normal. Yet these blues may be prolonged, impair functioning, and require treatment. The risk factors for depression during this period include a personal or family history of depression; chronic marital, family, or financial problems; a history of child abuse; youthful age; and medical complications during pregnancy.

Adequate treatment of depression is important not only for the health of the mother but also for the infant, as well as the other children in the family. There is good evidence that maternal depression impairs mother-infant bonding and may harm the child's later cognitive and emotional development. Infants of mothers depressed during pregnancy display poorer motor performance, dysregulated behavior, low birth weight, and prematurity (Grote, Bledsoe, Swartz, & Frank, 2004). Pregnancy is a good time for health interventions because pregnant women are already in the health care system if they are receiving prenatal care and certainly are during delivery and the postnatal period.

There has been considerable interest in treatment alternatives to medication for depression in the peripartum period to avoid the risk of possible harm to the fetus. Depressed women require treatment and are not likely to have spontaneous remission during pregnancy. Cohen et al. (2006) have shown the substantial risk of recurrence and relapse in pregnant depressed women who discontinue medication during pregnancy. However, Frank et al. (1990) demonstrated that even women with severely recurrent depression can be maintained in monthly maintenance IPT without medication for the length of their pregnancy.

Concerns about the possible effects of antidepressant medication on the developing fetus and the breast-fed infant have led to the exclusion of pregnant and breast-feeding postpartum women from antidepressant medication treatment trials. Although the effect of maternal antidepressant use on nursing infants is unclear, the American Academy of Pediatrics classifies most antidepressants as drugs whose effects on nursing mothers may be of concern.

Level of Evidence:

IPT during pregnancy: *** Validation by at least one randomized controlled trial or equivalent to a reference treatment of established efficacy

IPT for miscarriage: ** Encouraging findings in one or more open trials or in pilot studies with small samples

IPT during the postpartum period: ***

Adaptation

The adaptations of IPT needed to treat depression during pregnancy, miscarriage, and the postpartum period have been minimal (Spinelli & Endicott, 2003; O'Hara, Stuart, Gorman, & Wenzel, 2000; Neugebauer, Kline, Bleiberg, et al., 2006; Neugebauer, Kline, Markowitz, et al., 2006). The usual IPT problem areas nicely suit the issues that arise for women at these times. The birth of a child is a major role transition and may cause family disputes. Miscarriage is a time of grieving. The adaptations are:

1. *Differentiating depressive symptoms and symptoms of normal pregnancy:* There is an overlap between symptoms of depression and the symptoms associated with pregnancy and the postpartum period, particularly fatigue, appetite change, loss of energy, and sleep problems. It is useful to try to differentiate those that are the result of normal pregnancy from those that may be depressive in nature. In reviewing the symptoms, find out whether they began before or during pregnancy or in the postpartum period. For mild symptoms following childbirth, determine their impact on the mother's functioning and the duration and history of major depression.

2. *Interpersonal inventory:* To determine the triggers of the episode, explore the woman's feelings about the pregnancy, the baby, the father's role, whether it was a wanted pregnancy, what types of social supports are available, who is living in the house, and the ages of other children. A sexual and reproductive history, including previous miscarriages, difficulty in becoming pregnant, and use of IV fertilization, is also indicated. The interpersonal inventory is not altered.

3. *Flexibility in time:* Some modification of the timing and duration of the treatment may be necessary depending on the stage of the pregnancy. A flexible therapist should take into account the stage of pregnancy in which the woman presents for treatment, the expected time of delivery, and other family obligations. A break in therapy may be necessary around delivery and the brief postpartum period. On the other hand, if the woman remains seriously depressed and it is possible to telephone or meet with her during the obstetrical admission for delivery, such contact may cement the therapeutic alliance and provide relief during a potential crisis. There is substantial support for the use of the telephone to provide psychotherapy, including IPT (see Chapter 23).

If the woman agrees and would find it helpful, it is sometimes appropriate to involve other members of the family who may have substantial roles in the care of both the child and the mother during the pregnancy and postpartum period.

Less frequent visits following childbirth or the use of telephone sessions should sometimes be considered so that attending treatment sessions does not add to the new mother's burden. On the other hand, some women find therapy sessions a welcome break from the seemingly overwhelming responsibilities of child care.

The potentially positive impact on both the mother and the child of preventing or reducing depressive symptoms in pregnant and new mothers has led to several adaptations of IPT (Grote et al., 2004). A pilot study was successful in a four-session group IPT as compared to treatment as usual to reduce postpartum depression in pregnant women at high risk for major depression because of a previous history of depression and/or poor social supports (Zlotnick, Johnson, Miller, Pearlstein, & Howard, 2001). The four IPT sessions provided psychoeducation about new baby blues, discussed the role transition associated with the birth and ways to manage it, and, in the final session, focused on identifying and handling disputes.

Neugebauer, Kline, Bleiberg, et al. (2006) and Neugebauer, Kline, Markowitz, et al. (2006) successfully adapted a brief telephone version of IPT for women with subsyndromal depression postmiscarriage. By extension, IPT appears a reasonable intervention for women with full major depression postmiscarriage. The same issues apply: Was the pregnancy wanted? What is the woman's relationship with the father and other social supports? What was her experience of the miscarriage? Does she feel guilty? What were her expectations of life with the baby? The woman's sense of loss may relate to whether the miscarriage occurred early in pregnancy (before the quickening around week 20) or whether she had felt fetal kicking, had marked changes in her body, had begun furnishing a nursery, and so on. It is therefore helpful to learn about the timing of the miscarriage.

Problem Areas

The problem areas of IPT easily apply to pregnancy, miscarriage, and post-partum depression.

- *Grief:* Grief reactions may be due to a miscarriage or the mourning of a deceased child. A woman who has had a miscarriage, a stillborn child, or a child who died soon after birth must be helped through the grieving process as she would for any death. Grief in such cases often entails mourning not only the past but also the future the mother had imagined, the life she had hoped to have with her child.
- *Role disputes:* The postpartum period sometimes brings about numerous role disputes as the woman undertakes the care of the new infant, especially if she feels tired or overwhelmed. This is especially likely if the pregnancy was unwanted or the partner is absent or unsupportive. Disputes about autonomy and income might also arise for a woman who has had to give up her work in order to care for a child. If disputes do not arise in connection with giving up work, the change may still be a difficult role transition for many women. Disputes may arise with other children who feel jealous of the new baby and angry at the loss of attention from their mother.
- *Role transitions:* Pregnancy and the postpartum period are role transitions, especially in the instance of a first child. Transitions include giving up an outside work role or the loss of time and income.
- *Deficits:* As at other times, patients with interpersonal deficits (e.g., a paucity of relationships or attachments) can have a great deal of difficulty during this period and may require additional help in obtaining support from other family members, friends, or social service agencies in managing the burdens of child care. Yet pregnancy and delivery also inherently provide a new relationship for the patient to deal with, hence one of the other, preferable interpersonal problem areas should be invoked as a focus of treatment.
- *Complicated pregnancy:* Spinelli (1999) has identified a fifth area, "complicated pregnancy," in the case of rape, concurrent illness such as HIV, unplanned or untimely pregnancy, or a child born with anomalies. The clinician should be sensitive to the impact of these situations and become knowledgeable about them. The usual IPT problem areas apply to these pregnancy-related events.

13

Depression in Adolescents and Children

Adolescents

Background

Cross-national epidemiologic studies of the last two decades have found that major depression has an early onset, often in adolescence, and especially in girls. Untreated adolescent depression is associated with substantial morbidity including school dropout, teenage pregnancy, suicide attempts, and substance abuse, in addition to considerable health expenditures. Depression that begins in adolescence frequently continues into or recurs in adulthood (Weissman et al., 1999).

Adolescent depression is vastly undertreated: Less than a third of adolescents with mental health problems in the United States receive any mental health services. In recent years, school-based health clinics have emerged as an important treatment setting for adolescents with mental and general health problems, and some treatment studies have been conducted in these settings. IPT has been tested in a school-based clinic and modified to address the constraints of such a setting. Psychotherapy is an important treatment for depressed youth because of the controversy surrounding the use of psychotropic medications in this age group.

Depressed adolescents experience the range of *DSM-IV* depressive disorders, including major depression, dysthymic disorder, bipolar disorder, and depression not otherwise specified (NOS). The *DSM-IV* criteria can be used to diagnose depression in adolescents. The only difference is perhaps a predominance of irritability over depressed mood. Adolescents are also much more reactive than adults to external situations or stressors and may experience transient but acute episodes of depression, resolving in a few days. Yet the morbidity of even these transient episodes should not be underestimated. They often fluctuate with current life and interpersonal situations but can be impairing. Depressed adolescents carry a much higher risk for suicide attempts than adults or elderly people, and although these attempts may at times reflect a wish for attention rather than death, they can be serious or even lethal. Depression in adolescents is further significant because of its tendency to recur over the lifespan and to significantly impair psychosocial functioning, particularly if the adolescent is left untreated when important developmental educational or relationship tasks arise.

Being a patient undergoing treatment is an uncomfortable role for many people and is particularly uncomfortable for adolescents. Youthful patients may best tolerate a brief treatment that does not require a fixed number of sessions but is available as needed.

Level of Evidence: **** Validation by at least one randomized controlled trial or equivalent to a reference treatment of established efficacy

Adaptation

The prerequisite for therapists treating depressed adolescents with IPT is experience in working with depressed adolescents and in practicing IPT (Mufson, Pollack Dorta, Moreau, & Weissman, 2004; Mufson, Pollack Dorta, Wickramaratne, et al., 2004). IPT therapists generally take a relaxed and informal stance in conducting psychotherapy, but therapists working with this population must be comfortable in collaborating with teenagers. The adaptations that have been made for this age group are limited and concern the content of the IPT sessions, not the structure or techniques of the treatment. The content issue relates entirely to the developmental concerns of youth, not to any uniqueness of adolescent depression. Adaptations important for treating depressed adolescents with IPT are:

- *Flexibility:* The treatment should mesh with the adolescent's school schedule and other educational needs. Sessions, particularly if conducted in a school-based clinic, may need to be shortened to accommodate an academic schedule. Telephone sessions can be used to make up appointments missed due to scheduling conflicts. For a remitting youngster, attending basketball practice may be a sign of recovery rather than resistance to psychotherapy. This should be discussed and accepted.
- *The sick role:* The sick role in the initial phases of IPT can exempt the depressed patient from overly onerous responsibilities. The sick role is a state that, if chronic, would be socially undesirable and so should be resolved as quickly as possible. It labels the need for help. Except in rare, extreme cases, the sick role should not exempt the adolescent from attending school. It can accommodate lower grade performance or excusal from extracurricular activities, but school attendance must be maintained.
- *Involvement of parents or guardians:* Parents should be involved in the initial phase of treatment. The therapist makes seeing the parent a requirement of the adolescent's treatment. It is important to clarify to the patient that what is discussed in individual sessions will not be

conveyed to the parent unless there is a risk of suicide or harm to the adolescent or to a parent by the adolescent. Therapist contact with the parent is explained to the adolescent as the addition of another perspective on the adolescent's problems. During the initial phase, the therapist should meet with both the adolescent and a family member. Ideally everyone should meet together in order to explain the conduct of the initial evaluation and to discuss the goals of treatment. The therapist should explain to the parent the structure and overall content of the therapy sessions, the outline of IPT, the duration of treatment, and expectations of what will be discussed. To the extent possible (and this is not always possible), parents should be enlisted as facilitators rather than antagonists of the treatment, for their child's and their family's sake. In rare cases in which the parent refuses to be involved or the child refuses to have the parent involved, treatment should not be denied, but parental involvement should again be raised later in the treatment.

- *Outside information:* Relative to standard IPT, treatment with adolescents expands the sources of clinical information, including not only the adolescent but also parents, other family members, teachers, school personnel, and other health professionals or caretakers such as pediatricians and clergy. The therapist does not routinely seek clinical information from all of these sources but chooses as seems appropriate and relevant, guided by the content of the treatment sessions. For example, it might be appropriate to contact the teacher of an adolescent who is having school problems. This requires the adolescent's permission.

- *Confidentiality:* It is essential to discuss confidentiality with adolescents, as with all patients. The therapist guarantees that no discussion of the content of the sessions with parents or anyone else will take place unless the patient and therapist jointly decide that such communication would facilitate the treatment. The exception is if the adolescent is in danger: The therapist would then discuss breaching confidentiality with the patient before acting to make contact for the patient's safety. If possible, the parent should be updated in a general sense about the adolescent's progress (e.g., symptomatic improvement, attendance in therapy, recommendations to see a psychiatrist to consider medications). This contact should first be reviewed with the adolescent and approved. If the adolescent refuses to allow the therapist to speak to a parent, he or she should be encouraged to discuss such information with the parents directly.

Defining the Interpersonal Context

Obtaining information about the interpersonal context of depression and using the interpersonal inventory are similar in adolescents and adults.

Mufson, Pollack Dorta, Moreau, and colleagues (2004) graphically modified the interpersonal inventory for adolescents by using a visual "closeness circle" with an X in the middle, representing the patient. The patient is asked to place markers for significant relationships at appropriate distances from the X to illustrate their relative intimacy. This technique may be useful for adolescents who are having difficulty differentiating among relationships.

The events associated with depression in adolescents are age appropriate: typically, role transitions or disputes such as changes at school or in the family structure, the onset of sexuality, and sexual relations. These issues readily fit into the four problem areas used with adults. In an earlier version of IPT for adolescents a fifth problem area, single-parent family, was added, but subsequent experience has indicated that the issues within this category can be placed within disputes or transitions.

Depression Is a Family Affair

Depression is known to run in families. Quite commonly one or both of the adolescent's parents also suffer from depression or other related psychiatric disorders (e.g., alcohol or drug abuse). Many parents refuse interventions for themselves but encourage or allow the adolescent to accept treatment. On the other hand, parents may view the child's treatment in a negative light, perhaps because they had a course of unsuccessful treatment themselves. The more that parents can be involved in a successful course of an adolescent's treatment, the more likely they may be to enter treatment on their own. There is new evidence that successful treatment of a parent's depression to remission can reduce the child's symptoms as well (Weissman, Pilowsky, et al., 2006). Although the purpose of meeting with the parent is not primarily to assess the parent's clinical state, the therapist should be attuned to cues that may open up the topic. Caution is required in discussing the parents' psychopathology with the adolescent present.

Special Issues With Adolescents

Issues that arise in treating adolescents reflect their developmental phase. Some of special importance, which usually fall into the standard IPT problem areas, include nonnuclear or single-parent families, homosexuality, school refusal, sexual abuse, substance abuse, learning disabilities, sexual activity, birth control, and pregnancy. Mufson, Pollack Dorta, Moreau, et al. (2004) outline the specific handling of these situations.

Suicide Risk

Because suicidal thoughts and attempts are common among depressed adolescents, you should ask the adolescent directly:

Do you ever feel life is not worth living?
Do you think about death?
Do you wish you were dead?
Do you think about killing yourself?

Positive answers require a follow-up:

Have you ever made a suicide attempt? When? How? What happened?
Did you think you would die? Who was around when you did this? Did
you receive medical treatment? Did you tell anyone about it? Did your
parents know? What are you thinking about doing to hurt yourself? How
close are you? Will you be able to stop yourself? Will you be able to tell
someone before you hurt yourself?

The therapist must evaluate the degree of suicide risk, including lethality of plan, the adolescent's history, and the availability of a stable family and other social supports. A second opinion should readily be sought if you feel uncertain in determining the need for hospitalization. A possibly suicidal patient must be capable of establishing an alliance with the therapist. The therapist should feel confident that no suicidal plan will be carried out and that the adolescent will notify the therapist or go to the emergency room if the suicidal urges become compelling. Parents should be notified if the adolescent has a clear plan, will not form an alliance with the therapist, or cannot guarantee that the plan will not be carried out.

Prepubertal Depression

In contrast to adolescence, depression in school-aged prepubertal children (approximately ages 6–11 years) is fairly uncommon. The precise symptoms and clinical course are unclear at present. Few antidepressant treatments have been developed and tested for this age group. Pilowsky and Weissman (unpublished manual) have developed a manual adapting IPT for this age group. Since it has not been tested, we can recommend only that interested persons obtain and try it (see the list of manuals in the reference list for information on how to obtain it).

Level of Evidence: *(untested)

Adaptations

The two major adaptations are that most sessions involve the mother or caretaker along with the therapist and child and use play as part of the treatment. The assessment process may take longer for young children because of the child's limited insight and the need to gather information from multiple sources. Many of the problems that children face reflect their parents' interpersonal problems. Therefore, determination of the parents' clinical status and the emergence of current problems (grief, disputes, transitions) in the parents' lives often explain the reasons the child's symptoms have emerged and can be used to help the child in work with both the child and the parent. The recent data showing that successful treatment of a mother's depression can reduce the child's symptoms need to be considered in working with the parent (Weissman, Pilowsky, et al. 2006). While that study focused on the depressed mother, it is likely, albeit not tested, that the impact on the child of successfully treating the depressed father may also be considerable. In any case, when treating the child, awareness of the parents' current clinical state is important. What is clear from this study is that the absence of a father predicts a more difficult course for the depressed mother and her child.

14

Depression in Older Adults

Overview

Depression is one of the most common psychiatric diagnoses in older adults, but the first episode rarely occurs at this age. When it does, it may reflect an overwhelming stress, perhaps the loss of a spouse of many years or important social changes associated with retirement. However, the IPT therapist should also consider medical problems, including neurovascular disease, as the source of the patient's depressive symptoms. Most older patients with depression are experiencing a recurrence of previous episodes. The symptoms of depression are similar across the life cycle. However, older patients may focus more on physical symptoms, including somatic preoccupation, pain, and sleep disturbance.

The fact that older adults have more medical problems may complicate not only the diagnosis but also the treatment of depression. The onset of a disabling medical illness is a risk factor for depression. On the other hand, depression itself may be a contributing factor in different illnesses such as ischemic heart disease and stroke (Evans et al., 2005). Patients with both depression and cardiovascular disease or diabetes face an increased mortality risk (Gallo et al., 2005). Psychotherapy is an important modality for depressed older patients because they may have greater sensitivity to medication side effects and more difficulty tolerating antidepressants. Since they are often taking other medications, they may carry greater risk for drug interactions. On the other hand, Reynolds et al. (2006) have shown that depressed persons over 70 did better on medication than in IPT.

The biggest barrier to the use of IPT in depressed elderly people is often the belief of some therapists (contrary to the scientific evidence) that older patients do not do well in psychotherapy or are inflexible and cannot change. There is now ample evidence from controlled clinical trials that psychotherapy, particularly IPT, is a useful, efficacious, and accepted treatment in depressed elderly adults (Reynolds, III, Frank, Dew, et al., 1999; Hinrichsen & Clougherty, 2006). Case reports suggest that IPT can be used as an augmentative treatment in depressed elderly people who are responding poorly to an antidepressant drug (Scocco & Frank, 2002).

Reynolds and colleagues in Pittsburgh have conducted a series of maintenance IPT studies with older depressed patients. In each trial, they treated them with both IPT and a medication until their depression remitted and stabilized, then randomly assigned them to continued combined treatment, monotherapy with IPT or medication, or pill placebo. Patients aged 60–69 did best on the combination of IPT and medication, did well on monotherapy with either treatment alone, and relapsed quickly on placebo. Depressed patients aged 70 and older were more likely to relapse than patients aged 60–69 on monthly maintenance IPT alone compared to medication alone or in combination with IPT (Reynolds, III, Frank, Perel, et al., 1999; Reynolds, III, et al., 2006). The oldest patients had late onset major depressive disorder, and some may have suffered from early-stage Alzheimer's disease or vascular dementia. These findings suggest that elderly patients with their first onset in this age period may have a comorbid medical problem that compromises the effectiveness of psychotherapy and may require more involvement of caregivers.

Level of Evidence: **** Treatment has been validated by at least two randomized controlled trials demonstrating the superiority of IPT to a control condition.

Adaptation

As when dealing with any age or ethnic group, the clinician should understand the generational experiences that shape the values and worldview of the population under treatment: in this instance, the difficulties of later life, particularly retirement, medical problems, and bereavement.

Since depressive symptoms such as sleep and appetite disturbance, fatigue, and aches and pains overlap with many chronic medical illnesses, an older patient presenting for treatment of major depression should have a complete medical evaluation to rule out comorbid general medical illness that may account for the symptoms. *The presence of comorbid general medical disease does not mean that depression should not be treated:* It is not normal or expectable to develop major depression in the context of medical illness. Yet it is imperative, particularly for patients seeing nonmedical therapists, also to address other medical problems. Patients with pain or sleep disturbances take longer to remit in treatment (Karp et al., 2005). By contrast, there is no evidence that older patients, even those hospitalized for a medial illness (Mossey, Knott, Higgins, & Talerico, 1996), cannot tolerate 50-minute sessions, a finding at odds with impressions in earlier writings.

Problem Areas

The IPT problem areas generally apply to the common difficulties of aging. However, it is useful to understand how they nest within the IPT problem areas. For example:

- *Grief:* Elderly people face more experiences of bereavement. The most common one is the death of a spouse, partner, close friend, or relative. With the loss of a spouse, the patient must face not only the loss of a partner but also disruptions in the practical aspects of living. For a surviving spouse, bill payment, financial burdens, leisure activities, and relationships with children may change completely. These disturbances can lead to role disputes or transitions.

  Resolving grief reactions may be more complex than with younger patients, as older patients have more extended histories with the deceased person to discuss and resolve. The possibilities of meeting a new partner or interest in doing so may also be more limited. Insecurities about how to reenter the dating scene after many years in a stable relationship may contribute another element of distress. The compounding effect of additional deaths of friends, other relatives, or acquaintances around the same period of time, which is not unusual in this age group, may increase the patient's sense of vulnerability and exacerbate the symptoms of depression.

- *Interpersonal role disputes:* Some older adults have long-standing disputes with a spouse, partner, or adult children that are exacerbated by life changes such as retirement, financial problems, and the assumption of care for a family member. Issues and disputes with adult children often include disagreement over the frequency of visits or assistance or an adult child's mental health and substance use problems; unhappiness over the child's choice of spouse or partner, financial disagreements, or issues related to grandchildren.

- *Role transition:* Role transitions are common for older adults. Modal issues are the transition into the role of providing care to an infirm spouse or partner; transition to the role of an aging person with health problems and accompanying disability; retirement; or change of residence or community.

- *Interpersonal deficits:* This problem area is rarely identified in IPT with older adults. One explanation is that older adults often seek mental health services at the behest of a significant other, and persons with interpersonal deficits typically lack such close relationships. However, these people may come to the attention of staff when they enter assisted-living residency or long-term care facilities. Some older adults may find that the loss of a critical relationship such as a spouse or sibling confronts them with the reality that they have very limited social resources or experiences in obtaining new ones. In IPT this would be formulated as complicated bereavement if the significant other had died or as a role transition if the partner had moved away.

- *Medical model:* Older adults find the medical model of depression appealing since it is often familiar, given their other health problems. They may be less familiar with the view of depression as a medical illness and may need psychoeducation about depression and its treatment.

- *Interpersonal inventory:* Older adults have accumulated many relationships; hence the interpersonal inventory may take longer to complete. The focus should remain on the present insofar as possible, where the list of current relationships may be all too short.

- *Maintaining the IPT focus:* Cognitive researchers have described a phenomenon of "off-target verbosity" in older people and suggest this may be related to changes in the aging brain (Arbuckle, Nohara-LeClair, & Pushkar, 2000). This is reflected in the observations of IPT researchers that older depressed patients are more likely to reminisce about the past (Reynolds, III, Frank, Dew, et al., 1999). Clinically this can be addressed by initially clarifying to patients the framework of IPT and subsequently redirecting them to the relevant, agreed-upon focal problem area.

- *Therapist's view:* Therapists who have limited clinical experience working with older adults may be pessimistic about the likelihood of substantive change, daunted by patients' multiple medical problems, and discouraged by the sense that elderly individuals have limited options or abilities. Efficacy studies have found, however, that older, depressed adults are resilient, adaptive, and capable of change, and outcomes have been very positive in IPT (ibid.; APA Working Group on the Older Adult, 1998; Scogin & McElreath 1994). Psychotherapists who are treating geriatric patients thus need to fight ageism—negative therapeutic prejudices that depressed elderly patients themselves may well echo.

- *Physical accommodations and liaison with medical and social service agencies:* Older adults may need more concrete social services and are usually in medical treatment. Therefore it may be important, with the patient's permission, to contact the patient's physician to clarify problem areas. Older patients may need help in obtaining transportation to IPT sessions, temporary housing, and long-term care. Focusing on psychological issues can be a hollow pursuit when the basic activities of daily living are in disarray. The integration of these interventions may become more common when people age and are confronted with major role transitions that they cannot personally master.

- *Primary with cognitive impairment:* Miller et al. (2006) have modified IPT for elderly patients with cognitive impairment. This adaptation engages both patient and caregiver in treatment by giving psychoeducation to both, offering practice in solving problems for both parties individually, and providing a forum for role dispute resolution through joint meetings. Caregivers have regular input into the therapy and are encouraged to extend the work between meetings to help the patient maintain progress despite memory loss or impairment (ibid.). The efficacy of this approach has not yet been formally tested.

- *Primary care treatment of depression and suicidal ideation:* Because older patients frequently see a primary care physician, efforts have been made to treat depression and suicidal ideation in depressed, older, primary care patients (Alexopoulos et al., 2005). Treatment of suicidal ideation is important because suicide rates are highest in late life, and the majority of older adults who die by suicide have seen a primary care physician in the preceding 6 months. Depression is a strong risk factor for late-life suicide and its precursor, suicidal ideation. Elderly depressed patients who were offered case management that included IPT, when compared to patients receiving routine care, showed a decline in suicidal ideation over a 1-year period and a more favorable course of depression in both severity and speed of symptom reduction, changes that were significant at 4 months (Bruce et al., 2004). These results covered several primary care clinics and a range of ethnic groups in the United States. IPT was used for patients who declined medication and was administered for a year for acute continuation and maintenance treatment. The IPT therapists were master's-level clinicians. The dose of IPT was 12 weekly sessions during the first 3 months of acute treatment and monthly thereafter during the continuation phase of 6 months for patients showing some remission. Then, during a 15-month maintenance phase, IPT sessions were held bimonthly. If a patient relapsed, weekly sessions could resume. Interestingly, serotonin reuptake inhibitors (SSRIs) were considered the first-line treatment, and IPT was administered only if patients refused medication. Eleven percent of the patients initially requested IPT, but over a 12-month period, the prevalence of IPT as either monotherapy or augmentation of medication increased (Schulberg et al., in press).

Case Example: I Lost My Wife and My Life

Mr. D, a 66-year-old widower and retired lawyer, was brought to treatment by his family. He acknowledged being quite depressed in the aftermath of his wife's death from breast cancer 5 months earlier. On questioning, he stated that his depression had really begun when he retired from his job to care for her declining health a year and a half earlier. In fact, Mrs. D had been fighting breast cancer on and off for 8 years, an onslaught that he had described as having gradually taken over their lives. He was distracted from his work, and what he described as a previously warm and close relationship had suffered. "But why shouldn't I be depressed?" he asked. "My life is ruined, over."

He reported agitation, rumination, decreased sleep and appetite, a 15-pound weight loss, and passive suicidal ideation, with a sense that he might be reunited with his wife in death. His Hamilton Rating Scale for Depression score was 27.

Mr. D reported one prior episode of depression in his early twenties; he had also abused alcohol many years before but denied current use. He reported mild prostatic hypertrophy but was otherwise in good medical condition. He was adamant that he would not take an antidepressant medication.

Given a choice between a role transition based on retirement and complicated bereavement, both therapist and patient agreed to focus for 12 sessions on the latter. Mr. D felt guilty that he had let his wife down, believed that he should have cared for her better, and considered her the love of his life, an irreplaceable loss after some 40 years of marriage. The therapist encouraged him to reminisce about what he missed about Mrs. D and their marriage. She also noted that Mr. D had not discussed his feelings much with his friends and had not really used the available social supports. Mr. D stated that many friends and family members had either moved away or died in recent years, and he was not in any case one to talk about his feelings. He had withdrawn and kept to himself from the time of his wife's funeral. The therapist encouraged him to consider building new skills in this area, inasmuch as social supports could provide him with some comfort in his difficult situation.

As therapy continued, Mr. D reported that he had begun to attend synagogue for the first time in years and that his rabbi had provided some solace. At the same time, Mr. D began to discuss his ambivalent feelings about his wife—how her illness had distracted him from and ultimately ended his career and how she had annoyed him at times despite his wanting to care for her. Although they had had a wonderful marriage, there had (inevitably, his therapist noted) been some problems. He began to discuss these issues with a new level of affect, initially apologizing for his tears but gradually relaxing and accepting his feelings. His Hamilton score decreased to 13, and he began to become more socially active.

In the latter part of the 12-week therapy, Mr. D returned to the law, conducting pro bono work for senior citizens. He also became active as a volunteer for a local cancer society, raising funds and—somewhat to his surprise—developing new friends. Mr. D saw this cancer work as a tribute to his wife. He also reengaged with his children and other family members. By the end of treatment, his Hamilton Rating Scale for Depression score had fallen to 7. He was proud to have improved "by myself" without medication. Given his history, Mr. D and his therapist agreed to monthly maintenance IPT to help him preserve his gains.

15

Depression in Medical Patients

Overview

Depression often co-occurs with medical conditions such as cardiac disease, human immunodeficiency virus (HIV) infection, cancer, stroke, and diabetes (Evans et al., 2005). Data associate depression with adverse cardiac events such as heart attack, increased risk of hospitalization, and increased morbidity and death after bypass surgery or heart attack. Similarly, depression has been linked to accelerated immune system decline in HIV-positive women and poorer adherence to antiviral medications. Depression may lead patients to neglect treatment of other medical conditions; conversely, some Axis III syndromes may predispose to depression.

In the past, medical staff and many patients tended to consider depression as an expected consequence of medical illness: "Who wouldn't be depressed with cancer?" Yet most medically ill individuals are not depressed, and those who are often have histories of depression predating their medical illness. Most important, depression in the context of medical illness is usually treatable.

In recent years the detection and treatment of depression in medical patients has received increasing attention. Antidepressant medication is probably the most common treatment approach, mostly due to ease of administration and lack of trained therapists in most medical settings; however, there has also been increasing research and clinical interest in psychotherapy. Medical patients often have social and interpersonal distress associated with their illness, and some medical patients hesitate to take additional medication or face risks of interaction and side effects from adding psychotropic medication to their current medication regimes.

IPT has been tested and adapted for patients in primary care, as well as for patients with specific medical syndromes (Browne et al., 2002; Schulberg, Raue, & Rollman, 2002; Markowitz et al., 1998; Donnelly et al., 2000). It is being tested in depressed patients with coronary disease (Koszycki, Lafontaine, Frasure-Smith, Swenson, & Lesperance, 2004; Frasure-Smith et al., 2006; see Caron & Weissman, 2006, for review), as well as somatizing patients in medical settings (Stuart & Noyes Jr., in press).

Because of the pressured nature of current medical practice and because patients who come primarily for treatment of general medical conditions may have less interest in longer-term psychotherapy (even 16 weeks), there have been efforts to decrease the number, as well as the length, of IPT sessions. An abbreviated form of IPT called interpersonal counseling (IPC) has been developed and tested (Weissman & Klerman, 1986; see reference list for manuals).

Interpersonal problem areas are relevant to the experience of medical illness. Receiving the diagnosis of a serious illness constitutes a role transition, one that can involve changes in physical appearance, loss of work or productivity, change in familial responsibility, or the loss of an extended future and anticipatory mourning of one's own approaching death. The role transition of medical illness may isolate the patient from social supports. Medical illnesses can produce interpersonal disputes with medical staff and family members.

Level of Evidence

> IPT in medical patients: **** Treatment has been validated by at least two randomized controlled trials demonstrating the superiority of IPT to a control condition.

> IPC in medical patients: *** Validation by at least one randomized controlled trial or equivalent to a reference treatment of established efficacy

Adaptation

With medical patients, the need for flexibility in scheduling is critical so as not to conflict with medical visits. If possible, therapists should schedule sessions in the hospital if the patient is admitted or on the telephone if the patient is incapacitated by illness or just prefers telephone contact (see Chapter 23). Adjusting in these ways to the patient's suffering and needs frequently consolidates the therapeutic alliance with those who may fear abandonment. Therapists and patients face confusion about whether somatic symptoms derive from depression or the medical comorbidity. In the case of HIV and depression, treating the depression has often alleviated fatigue, insomnia, and poor concentration that both therapist and patient had attributed to HIV infection (Markowitz et al., 1998). The interpersonal inventory should explore family histories of illness and medical treatment, as well as the patient's own experience with medicine.

Patients with serious or incapacitating medical regimes (e.g., cancer patients undergoing chemotherapy appear to appreciate the use of telephone sessions [Donnelly et al., 2000]). When families are involved, it may be helpful in the initial phase to educate both the family and the patient about the medical regime the patient is undergoing. This has been useful in the treatment of cancer chemotherapy patients, where the family and the patient had many questions about the course of illness and disability and needed additional social services to help maintain family functioning and arrange transportation.

Some research groups have suggested that the available patient guide and monitoring forms can be sent to patients before treatment begins in order to maximize the therapeutic effect and teach patients who are not coming primarily for psychiatric treatment what to expect in the psychotherapy (Weissman, 2005).

Other researchers have abbreviated IPT to fewer sessions (6–8) while maintaining the basic structure of the treatment. IPT has been tested with patients with subsyndromal depression with stable coronary artery disease (Frasure-Smith et al., 2006), with depressed patients with HIV infection and AIDS (Markowitz et al., 1998), and with breast cancer patients (Donnelly et al., 2000). In the adaptation for HIV patients, therapists told patients that they had two medical illnesses, depression and HIV, and adapted the sick role and psychoeducation to include both.

Primary Care and Elderly People

Because elderly people frequently attend primary care clinics, detection and treatment of depression in this setting is possible (Alexopoulos et al., 2005; Schulberg et al., in press; Bruce et al., 2004). (See Chapter 14 on older adults for the description of management with IPT.)

Case Example: Diabetes Was Not the Only Problem

Len, a 21-year-old college student, was admitted to the hospital with his fourth episode of diabetic ketoacidosis. His chief complaint was "I've had it."

Since Len's diagnosis with diabetes mellitus 3 years before, near the start of his freshman year of college, both his sugar and his emotions had been out of control. Despite the pleas of his doctors, parents, and friends, he had refused to follow a diet, test his blood sugar, or take insulin regularly. His glycosylated hemoglobin (A1c) level was 9%. The normal range (that found in healthy persons) is 4–5.9%.

On evaluation, Len appeared both angry and despairing. He reported neurovegetative symptoms of depression, including changes in sleep, appetite, weight, and energy level. It was difficult, however, to determine how much of this was attributable to a mood disorder and how much to his endocrine status. He reported feeling hopeless, helpless, and worthless and believed that he was defective and that his life was over. "College is supposed to be partying, girls, and beer," he said. "The doctors tell me I'm not allowed to drink like I want to. And who's going to go out with a damaged freak like me?" He felt diabetes had ruined his college experience, his body, and his life. He had alienated most of his few friends on campus and was failing his courses. He wanted to die and seemed to have invited his diabetic crises on occasion with sporadic drinking binges. His Hamilton Rating Scale for Depression score was 22.

Len refused to take antidepressant medication because he was against medications altogether. He did, however, vent his feelings to the consultation-liaison psychiatrist, who validated Len's anger and frustration about his condition. "No wonder you're depressed," said the therapist. They began to discuss the social and career expectations Len had brought to college and how "this sugar bit" had shattered them. In the second session, the therapist reinforced the diagnosis of major depression, showed Len a pocket *DSM-IV,* and linked the depression to the *role transition of a major medical illness*—diabetes mellitus. "You have two related medical problems, and either one can kill you if you don't take care of them. On the other hand, we can work on treating these problems, both of which can get in your way but neither of which is untreatable or your fault. If you can get them under control, you can live more of the life you had wanted."

Once Len's blood sugar was acutely controlled in the hospital with diet and insulin, he was discharged to outpatient follow-up in continuing IPT with the same psychiatrist. They agreed to a 12-week course of treatment focusing on resurrecting Len's college life. In the sessions, Len mourned his loss of health, the imposition of a strict schedule on what had been a pleasantly slovenly life, and his sense that the diabetes made him unattractive to women. He felt that the illness was "forcing me to grow up" prematurely: College was supposed to be the end of youth, not the beginning of adulthood. The therapist agreed that Len had put his finger on the role transition he faced: He had lost an innocent, "party animal" role and had to grow up faster than he wanted to. That was sad, frustrating, and enraging. He had definitely lost something, and it was appropriate to be upset. But was there anything good about the new role he had to adapt to?

Len mentioned that, despite his hostility toward doctors and hospitals, he had started to feel some interest in his illness and had thought about shifting his concentration from prelaw to premed. However, with his sugar out of control, he had trouble concentrating in class and studying, so the idea seemed unrealistic. The therapist encouraged this interest and urged Len to become expert both about diabetes and depression. Len got his roommate to remind him to check his blood sugar and to snack more regularly. His concentration and study habits began to improve.

Yet Len's overriding concern was his social life. He felt that diabetes was taking from him the drinking and partying that had been the focus of his college dreams and the only comfortable venue in which to meet women. He and his therapist began to talk about his feelings of inadequacy around women—which had predated his diagnosis of diabetes—and to role-play interactions in nondrinking situations. With the therapist's encouragement, Len began to make overtures to women in his classes and in other activities such as pick-up Ultimate Frisbee games. Not all of these encounters went smoothly, but enough did that he began to feel more confident and to date.

As this occurred, Len became less depressed and more willing to take care of his diabetes. At the end of 12 weeks, he was doing better on medical, academic, and social fronts. He drank only rarely and in moderation, and his Ham-D score had fallen to 7 and his hemoglobin A1c to 4%, both in the normal range. He now described himself as a more adult diabetes "survivor."

Interpersonal Counseling

In recognition of the temporal, physical, and personnel barriers to implementing weekly psychotherapy in medical settings, Weissman and Klerman developed a briefer psychosocial intervention based on IPT: interpersonal counseling (IPC) (Weissman & Klerman, 1986; Klerman et al., 1987). Other investigators have also studied this approach (Neugebauer, Kline, Bleiberg, et al., 2006; Neugebauer, Kline, Markowitz, et al., 2006; Mossey et al., 1996; Judd, Piterman, Cockram, McCall, & Weissman, 2001; Judd, Weissman, Davis, Hodgins, & Piterman, 2004). This brief intervention is useful because the availability of mental health personnel is limited in primary care settings, and patients often do not present primarily for psychological treatment. IPC is a simplified version of IPT that can be administered by non–mental health professionals and is intended for subsyndromal depression.

IPC involves both fewer and briefer sessions, up to six sessions of 15–30 minutes each, with the number determined by the patient as treatment progresses. IPC addresses current stressors, and patients may decide to end treatment after fewer than six sessions if they have made adequate progress. To aid non–mental health practitioners in its use, IPC scripts for each session have been outlined and homework added to facilitate treatment. IPC has been used with medically ill, hospitalized elderly patients for 10 sessions, administered by psychiatric clinical nurse specialists (Mossey et al., 1996), and, in Australia, by general practitioners in combination with a medication in a primary care setting (Judd et al., 2001, 2004). The management of stress, distress, and depression in patients in medical treatment is important, but the format must be easy to learn, sufficiently simple for administration by nonmedical personnel without psychotherapy experience, and flexible enough to combine with primary medical treatment and accommodate a patient's compromised energy. For patients with comorbid medical conditions, it is important to rule out the medical illness as the explanation for the symptom. For patients who deny distress or psychopathological symptoms associated with the medical condition, therapists may suggest that some of their symptoms extend beyond and compound the medical condition and may be helped by psychotherapy.

IPC is best applied with patients who have low levels of depressive symptoms and where trained therapists are not available but health personnel are interested in providing counseling. Direct testing comparing IPT to IPC has not been attempted.

16

Dysthymic Disorder

Diagnosis

Dysthymic disorder is a syndrome similar to major depression, generally of slightly lower symptomatic intensity but of longer duration. The severity of symptoms may not reach the threshold for major depressive disorder (MDD; when it does, it is called "double depression"), but symptoms typically begin early in life and continue for decades. The *DSM-IV* criteria for duration require a minimum of 2 years (1 year in adolescents) with no more than 2 months of relief, but patients frequently report having felt miserable for their entire lives, with no more than a day or two of improvement here or there.

This chronic debility takes a toll not only in constant dysphoria but also in impaired psychosocial functioning. Individuals who became depressed in childhood or adolescence may never have learned appropriate interpersonal skills, and those who did may have seen them erode in subsequent years of suffering. They tend to have limited social supports and few confidants. They often believe that their depressed mood is part of their personality, rather than a symptom that can be successfully treated.

All of the interpersonal issues typically seen in major depressive disorder tend to be exaggerated for dysthymic or other chronically depressed patients: social withdrawal, passivity, difficulty with self-assertion and confrontation, the sense that expressing needs is selfish and that anger is a "bad" emotion. These individuals have recognized that other people do not want to hear about chronic suffering, so they typically put on as bright a front as they can, shunning the spotlight and trying to pass as "normal." If they then succeed in some aspect of life, they tend to feel that they are frauds.

Because dysthymic symptoms are chronic and indolent, people with dysthymia can often use all of their limited energy and eke out adequate work functioning. If an episode of major depression does not occur, these people may avoid treatment, believing that the problem is simply their personality. Alternatively, individuals with dysthymia may have sought long-term psychotherapy for character change—a setting in which they have been reputed to have a poor prognosis—and have achieved little change in mood or social functioning.

Patients with dysthymia often avoid intimate relationships or feel unable to form such attachments, fearing that closeness will reveal to the other person how defective, fraudulent, or unlovable the patient is.

Level of Evidence:

> IPT alone: no stars. IPT has been found to be no better than a control condition as monotherapy.
>
> IPT as a combined treatment with medication: ** Encouraging findings in one or more open trials or in pilot studies with small samples.

Chronic depression is considered harder to treat than acute depression. Pharmacotherapy is the best proven single treatment for dysthymic disorder and other forms of chronic depression. IPT with patients with dysthymia has been tested in two clinical trials. In one, 94 patients with pure dysthymic disorder were randomly assigned to brief supportive psychotherapy (BSP), sertraline, or sertraline and IPT and were compared for 16 weeks (Markowitz et al., 2005). Patients improved in all conditions. The study was underpowered, but medication was superior to the other treatments in achieving response and remission. IPT and brief supportive therapy had equivalent outcomes. The degree of change that IPT patients made in their focal interpersonal problem areas correlated with the degree of symptomatic improvement (Markowitz, Bleiberg, Christos, & Levitan, 2006).

Another large trial randomly assigned 707 patients with dysthymic disorder or double depression to receive IPT (not modified for dysthymic disorder), sertraline, or a combination of both (Browne et al., 2002). Unfortunately, the IPT treatment consisted of 12 sessions, whereas medication was continued for more than 2 years, a somewhat unbalanced comparison. The investigators reported a 47% response rate for IPT alone, significantly less than the 60% rate for sertraline alone and 57.5% for combined treatment. Yet IPT was found to be associated with lower health and social service costs, rendering combined treatment most cost effective (ibid.). IPT actually performed well in this study considering the dosage disparity between IPT and sertraline. Nonetheless, this trial did not technically demonstrate efficacy for IPT.

Two other studies provide some support for IPT as an augmentation of medication for patients with dysthymia. In one small trial, chronically depressed patients who received the antidepressant medication moclobemide plus IPT had somewhat better outcomes than those who received moclobemide alone (Feijó de Mello, Myczowisk, & Menezes, 2001). In the other, patients responding to fluoxetine showed suggestions of greater benefits when given a group therapy combining interpersonal and cognitive interventions for depression than those who received fluoxetine alone (Hellerstein et al., 2001).

These results suggest that medication is the first-line treatment for dysthymic disorder. Psychotherapy, including IPT, may be a useful adjunct and would seem to target important interpersonal difficulties endemic to the disorder, but strong evidence for efficacy of IPT is lacking.

Yet for some patients with dysthymia who do not want to take or do not respond to medication, IPT may be an alternative treatment. Further modification of the IPT manual for dysthymic disorder may be helpful. IPT remains to be systematically tested in patients with both dysthymic disorder and MDD. Since IPT-D did not fare badly in the trials described and there are methodological problems (e.g., changes in therapist personnel during the trial) that may have hurt its chances, IPT still should not be dismissed as a potential sole treatment for patients with dysthymia. Based on clinical experience and preliminary data (Markowitz, 1993; Feijó de Mello et al., 2001), IPT may be helpful for chronically depressed patients who respond to medication and feel better but find themselves lacking in the interpersonal skills needed to conduct a euthymic life, skills that have either atrophied or never developed in the setting of chronic depression.

For these reasons, this chapter describes the adaptations of IPT for the treatment of patients with dysthymic disorder (Markowitz, 1998; see manual list in the references). Some of these adaptations may also apply to other chronic psychiatric syndromes such as social anxiety disorder (Chapter 20).

Adaptation

Although the IPT approach to dysthymic disorder generally resembles the treatment of major depression, there are several important changes.

Chronic IPT Model

The usual IPT model connects a recent temporal event in the patient's interpersonal life with current mood and symptoms. For patients who have been depressed for many years or for as long as they can remember, this model makes less sense: Even if there has been a recent, upsetting life event, this does not explain years of suffering. Hence for such patients we have developed the concept of an *iatrogenic role transition,* that is, a transition initiated by the doctor, in which the patient moves from recognition of illness to health and from psychosocial functioning impaired by dysthymic disorder to better functioning and mood. This transition takes advantage of patients' confusion between who they are and their long-standing mood disorder, which after so many years they may naturally confuse with their personality. The IPT therapist makes treatment itself a role transition in which the patient learns to recognize depressive symptoms of long duration and how they have affected their social functioning. In addition, they learn to handle interpersonal situations in a euthymic, nondepressed fashion. Learning such new ways of managing interpersonal interactions in a healthy way should lead to improved mood and self-esteem.

The therapist takes a careful history and an interpersonal inventory, look-ing for patterns in relationships and for good relationships and strengths the patient may have shown. Patterns to expect in chronic depression include shyness (avoidant personality traits), passivity (particularly in social situations; less so in situations defined by a job description), discomfort with self-asser-tion, anger, confrontation, and social risk taking.

The therapist then offers a formulation:

> *As we've discussed, you are suffering from dysthymic disorder, a chronic form of depression. It's a treatable illness, and it's not your fault. You have been depressed for so long that you very naturally have trouble distinguish-ing depression from who you are: You think it's your personality, but it isn't. You just have been depressed for so long that you can't tell the difference. Dysthymic disorder has to make it harder to handle social situations: Social discomfort is a hallmark of the condition.*
>
> *I suggest that we spend the next 16 weeks helping you to figure out what depression is and what you might be like when not depressed. If you can learn to handle situations in your life in a nondepressed way, not only should that make life go better, but you're also likely to feel better and more in control. And then maybe you'll begin to see that what you're suffering from is a treatable depression, not your personality.*

With the patient's acceptance of this formulation, treatment proceeds. Therapists work hard with such patients to identify emotions—and particu-larly negative affect, feelings of competitiveness, anger, sadness—that arise in everyday situations. Therapist and patient discuss whether such feelings are understandable and warranted. The idea of a *transgression*—that there are some behaviors that break expected social conduct, warrant anger, and de-serve at the least an apology—may be helpful in normalizing such feelings for patients (see Chapter 9):

> *If you're selfish all of the time, that's a problem. But if you're selfless all of the time, you're a martyr, and you're going to have trouble getting what you want and need. Everyone does better if they are a little selfish; if you don't speak up on your own behalf, who will?*

Once feelings are identified and normalized, a lot of role-play is often needed to help patients become comfortable with self-assertion or confron-tation. Yet if a patient has a success experience in one of these situations (e.g., asking for and receiving a raise, confronting a spouse), the patient will have learned a new skill, discover some sense of control over the local environment, and likely feel better.

The adaptation of IPT-D includes 16 weekly sessions to drive these points home. Patients who improve are still likely to feel shaky: After what may be four decades of depression, a few weeks of feeling better is unlikely to instill a feeling of security. For this reason we have routinely offered monthly con-tinuation sessions and sometimes maintenance therapy (Chapter 11). In our experience, it takes several months for patients' euthymic self-image and new track record of healthy interpersonal functioning to sink in and for them to believe they are really better.

Case Example: Taking All of the Blame

Ms. D, a 53-year-old woman, sought treatment because "My husband is disgusted with me." She reported having always felt sad, shy, and inferior. She completed college and had worked briefly before marrying a high-powered executive who expected her to run the house and care for their three children, one of whom, Kayla, had major developmental problems. She saw Kayla's problems as her own failure.

Ms. D presented for treatment with double depression when her two other children were leaving home and she was left with her increasingly handicapped daughter and her angry, unsupportive spouse. She felt indignant about the way her family treated her but felt that anger was a "bad" emotion that confirmed what a damaged person she was. She tended to comply and suffer silently, meeting other people's needs at the sacrifice of her own. Indeed, she was hard pressed to state what her own needs were. She had few social supports outside of her immediate family. She had had numerous prior trials of antidepressant medication with little benefit. She similarly had felt a two-year supportive psychodynamic psychotherapy, which had focused on understanding her childhood more than her current problems, was a waste of time and money, although she had never told the therapist this.

In the initial session, Ms. D's therapist diagnosed dysthymic disorder that had worsened into major depression. He noted her Hamilton Rating Scale for Depression score of 23 as evidence of this. The therapist then suggested that they spend the next 15 weeks (for a total of 16 sessions) looking at how chronic depression was affecting her life and her interactions with important people in her life. He explained dysthymic disorder as a condition from which she had suffered for so long that she seemed to consider it part of herself. He also stated, however, that she could learn in therapy to distinguish herself from the depression. Therapy was defined as a role transition to health.

Ms. D was skeptical but compliant. Early sessions focused on identifying and validating emotions such as her resentment of her husband and recasting them as useful and appropriate signals of frustrating situations. This took longer than it would have in treating acute depression, but after a couple of sessions she was able to tentatively role-play expressing such feelings. She and the therapist tried to anticipate how her husband might respond: with anger, interruptions, denials. Then, with trepidation she began to try to set protective limits ("as self-defense") with her husband and handicapped daughter. They also explored Ms. D's needs and discussed whether she needed to feel "selfish" in pursuing them.

D: So, I guess I should talk to Jack about his helping with Kayla, but it's not going to work.

THERAPIST: What would you want him to do? What would be helpful to you?

D: I'd like him to really understand how hard it can be to live with her. He's never home, and when he is, the kids are my responsibility. . . . It's my fault for not bringing her up better; that's why she's having these problems. I know we've discussed that I blame myself because I'm depressed, but he blames me, too.

THERAPIST: Do you agree? Is that fair?

D: Sometimes I get confused. But no, I guess I more and more don't think it's fair. The psychologists say that we didn't do anything wrong to Kayla.

THERAPIST: So how do you feel when Jack blames you?

D: Angry? I don't like that feeling. But yes, it feels unfair. I resent it.

THERAPIST: And do you think that's a reasonable feeling?

D: I don't like the feeling. But yes, it's called for.

THERAPIST: So what options do you have in dealing with Jack?

D: It hasn't felt like there were any options. I guess—I guess I could say what I just said. That Kayla's problems aren't my fault and that I resent it when he blames me. We should work together to try to help her. That would be best for all of us.

THERAPIST: How did that sound?

D: Pretty good, I guess.

THERAPIST: Is there something you would say differently? Did you say what you wanted to say? . . . Were you happy with your tone of voice?

D: Yes, but he'll probably not even let me finish. On the rare occasion when I start to say something, he cuts me off.

THERAPIST: Let's talk about what you would specifically like Jack to do to help you out and also about how you can handle it if he should interrupt.

To Ms. D's surprise, her husband listened to her feelings without interrupting. He told her for the first time how much he respected her handling of Kayla's difficult behaviors and offered to provide more help around the house. Although he briefly became irritated, Ms. D was able to tolerate this, and overall their encounter went far better than she had expected. Her mood improved, and her Hamilton depression score fell to 13. She was then willing to make further efforts to confront her family members and to gratify her own wishes in small ways. By the end of treatment, Ms. D was shakily euthymic, with a Hamilton score of 8. She eagerly consented to monthly follow-up sessions for the ensuing 6 months, during which period she maintained her euthymia (Ham-D = 5 after 6 months) and began to consolidate her nondepressed track record and identity. She developed new friendships and independent interests outside of her home. She remained improved on a 2-year follow-up.

This patient was not treated with medication, but many patients with dysthymia will respond best to the combination of medication and psycho-therapy. In such instances, an antidepressant medication can relieve the symptoms of dysthymic disorder, freeing the patient to work on interpersonal issues in IPT-D.

17

Bipolar Disorder

Diagnosis

Bipolar disorder has long been recognized as a serious psychiatric disorder. The treating clinician should be familiar with the symptoms of mania as well as depression (see Chapter 2). Most bipolar patients present for treatment during the depressive phase of the disorder, but a history of manic symptoms should be obtained even with currently depressed patients. Because bipolar patients require special attention, nonmedical clinicians should always consult with a psychiatrist if a manic history is suspected to clarify the diagnosis and to introduce or monitor medication. The risk of suicide and social disruption in family and work situations is high for individuals with bipolar disorder. When patients are manic, they are reluctant to stay on medication or remain in any treatment.

Until recently, treatment research had focused almost exclusively on pharmacotherapy. There is no question that pharmacotherapy is essential to the treatment of bipolar I disorder (BPI); less is known about bipolar II disorder. In the last few years, research has explored the utility of psychotherapies as adjuncts to pharmacotherapy for bipolar patients. There are clinical reasons to expect that psychotherapy might be useful to these patients. Bipolar disorder is a profoundly dislocating condition, disrupting relationships through its depressive, manic, and psychotic symptoms. Patients often emerge from episodes with their sense of self shattered and their life situation in upheaval. Moreover, life events can trigger new episodes of depression or mania. Recent evidence suggests that Interpersonal and Social Rhythm Therapy (IPSRT), an amalgamation of IPT with behavioral therapy, is an efficacious adjunct to medication for patients with bipolar I disorder. The behavioral component addresses coordination and stabilization of daily behaviors, especially the preservation of sleep, which is a critical factor in avoiding manic episodes.

> Level of Evidence: *** Validation by at least one randomized controlled trial or equivalent to a reference treatment of established efficacy

In a randomized clinical trial of 175 patients with bipolar I, Frank and colleagues (2005) found that mood-stabilizing medication was more efficacious in combination with IPSRT (Frank et al., 2005) than when administered in an intensive clinical management (ICM) control condition. The study was complex, with a design involving dual randomization to IPSRT or ICM at both the acute and maintenance phases of treatment. Initial time to stabilization did not differ between IPSRT and ICM, although IPSRT patients regularized their social rhythms more in the acute phase (Frank et al., 2005).

Patients treated with acute IPSRT remained euthymic longer in the maintenance phase before developing a recurrent episode, regardless of whether they received IPT or ICM in the maintenance phase. Ability to increase the regularity of social rhythms using IPSRT during the acute phase was also associated with reduced likelihood of recurrence during the maintenance phase. This suggested that early introduction of IPT and social rhythm therapy for BPI in the acute phase has a prophylactic benefit. However, bipolar patients with multiple medical problems took longer to reach remission and fared better in ICM (which focused on the patient's somatic symptoms) than in IPSRT. In contrast, IPT focused on increasing the social stability of patients' lives (Frank et al., 2005). Finally, patients with comorbid panic disorder had a poorer outcome.

Adaptation

This is the first IPT adaptation to be designed as an adjunct to medication, rather than as a stand-alone, primary treatment; it is also the first attempt to integrate IPT with a behavioral approach.

The problem in adapting IPT to bipolar disorder lay not with the depressive phase of the disorder, for which IPT approaches were already well developed, but with the mania. Frank and colleagues in Pittsburgh recognized that a crucial aspect of mania was the disruption of the diurnal life schedule, particularly the loss of sleep, which commonly triggers mania. Accordingly, they developed a behavioral approach to regularize daily social activities (especially sleep). Patients fill out a weekly grid of activities, the Social Rhythm Metric (SRM), starting each morning and running throughout the day, to mark social anchors of daily routines. They review the SRM with therapists to see how regular their schedule is, how stimulating activities are (how many people they encounter at breakfast, etc.), and what sorts of things may be interfering with a predictable, organized day and night. Focusing on such daily behavioral patterns can enable patients to regularize their schedules, thus decreasing the likelihood of a student pulling an all-nighter, for example, and provoking a manic episode (Frank, Swartz, & Kupfer, 2000). IPT does not attempt to treat mania once it has arisen—when patients are unlikely to listen to or collaborate with therapists—but rather to prevent its recurrence.

The depressive phase of bipolar illness is treated much as it is for unipolar depression. The usual concomitants of depression arise with complicated bereavement, role disputes, and role transitions associated with depressive episodes. An additional interpersonal focus has been added: "grief for the lost healthy self." This concept encompasses the reality that patients may remit from a severe manic or depressive episode to find their lives in shambles. They need to grieve and come to terms with the effect their illness has wrought on their lives. This would seem to be a special case of a role transition.

Case Example: Taming the Roller Coaster

Ms. B, a 28-year-old woman, presented for treatment with bipolar II disorder. She felt depressed much of the time and became hypomanic under stress, resulting in impulsive behavior and mild overspending. On presentation, her Hamilton Rating Scale for Depression score was 23 (moderately depressed). Stressors in her life included job pressures and a conflicted sexual relationship of two years with an older, married celebrity. Her work in a publishing house prompted frequent all-nighters to meet copy deadlines, a pattern that disrupted her sleep schedule and her mood. Ms. B reported that her mother had been diagnosed with manic depression and had responded well to lithium. She herself had seen psychiatrists in the past but had been put off by their emphasis on medication, which she feared taking.

Her therapist gave Ms. B the diagnosis of bipolar II disorder and explained its risks and potential treatments. The therapist pointed out that bipolar II was a lifelong but treatable illness; he suggested a 12-week IPSRT treatment with likely maintenance treatment if acute treatment was beneficial. He also emphasized that, while acute treatment was important, the goal of therapy was the general stabilization of mood and reduction of both depressive and hypomanic episodes over time, what the patient termed "taming the roller coaster."

Ms. B was reluctant to take lithium like her mother but did accept another medication, which seemed to provide partial relief of her symptoms; nonetheless, she remained depressed much of the time and still reported a tendency toward hypomania. Using the Social Rhythm Metric (see Table 17.1), she and her therapist reviewed her erratic sleep schedule and discussed good "sleep hygiene": slowing down in the evening, avoiding caffeine and alcohol, conducting only relaxing activities in the hours before bedtime, and going to bed and arising at the same regular hours. They discussed what work options Ms. B had to avoid all-nighters, which she decided she could minimize by spacing out her work assignments and not procrastinating.

In the meantime, the therapist noted that the patient's depression often seemed related not to Ms. B's work, which she loved, but to her relationship with her "VIP lover," C. They defined this as a role dispute. Ms. B tended to take a subservient role in this relationship but felt neglected and misunderstood. Taking the standard role dispute approach, both patient and therapist explored Ms. B's positive and negative feelings about C and their relationship, what she wanted from it, and how she could achieve her wishes. Except during hypomanic moments, Ms. B was extremely passive in the relationship and had great difficulty either expressing her needs or setting limits with C.

Using the SRM, Ms. B was able to organize and regularize her sleep and activity schedule. She had initially been skeptical of how helpful this would be but conceded that it made a difference in her mood and energy level. With considerable role-playing, she was able to express her wishes to C more fully; he was not entirely receptive but respected her opinions and met her halfway on some wishes, such as taking a vacation together, which the patient considered a huge achievement. Her Hamilton Depression scale score had fallen to 9 by the end of 12 sessions. Ms. B then contracted for 2 years of monthly maintenance sessions (see Chapter 11), through which she has remained minimally depressed and without hypomanic episodes.

Comment Based on a single, large study, ISPRT appears to be an important development in the treatment of bipolar I disorder as an adjunct to mood-stabilizing medication. Its effects without medication are unknown. Frank et al. (2005) treated patients for 2 years, but bipolar illness is lifelong, and continual treatment is indicated. The application of IPSRT to bipolar II disorder warrants study.

Table 17.1   Social Rhythm Metric II, Five-Item Version (SRM-II-5)

Week of _____

Directions:

1. Write the *ideal target time* you would *like* to do these daily activities.
2. Record the *time* you actually did the activity each day.
3. Record the *people* involved in the activity: 0 = alone; 1 = others present; 2 = others actively involved; 3 = others very stimulating

Activity	Target Time	Sunday Time/P*	Monday Time/P	Tuesday Time/P	Wednesday Time/P	Thursday Time/P	Friday Time/P	Saturday Time/P
Out of bed								
First contact with another person								
Start work/ school/ volunteer/ family care								
Dinner								
To bed								
Rate mood daily from −5 (very depressed) to +5 (very elated)								

Rate mood daily from −5 (very depressed) to +5 (very elated)

*P = Number of people present

Adapted from E. Frank, *Treating Bipolar Disorder* (2005)

Section III
Adaptations of IPT for Non–Mood Disorders

18

Substance Abuse

In addition to substance-induced disorders, the category of substance use disorders comprises dependence on and abuse of substances such as alcohol, opiates, cocaine, and nicotine. Substance abuse and dependence are prevalent, debilitating conditions. They often leave a trail of broken relationships and eroded social skills. Hence sobriety is a role transition that might fit the IPT model since it requires the rebuilding of social skills, relationships, and life roles that substance use has devastated (Cherry & Markowitz, 1996). Unfortunately, the available data do not allow us to recommend IPT as a treatment for patients whose focus of the treatment is a substance use disorder.

There have been two negative IPT trials with drug-abusing patients and no trials in alcohol use disorders. In one, IPT was added to a standard drug program psychosocial intervention to reduce psychopathology among 72 methadone-maintained, opiate-dependent patients (Rounsaville, Glazer, Wilber, Weissman, & Kleber, 1983). Both treatment groups improved, but there was no advantage found for adding IPT. Since all of the patients were already receiving good substance abuse treatment and psychotherapy, this raises the issue of a ceiling effect, and it is hard to show differences between effective treatments.

IPT was also ineffective in helping intravenous cocaine–dependent patients in achieving cocaine abstinence (Carroll, Rounsaville, & Gawin, 1991). In that 12-week study, IPT was compared to a behavioral therapy. Both were characterized by high dropout and poor response; there was no suggestion of an advantage for IPT.

We are currently analyzing data from a small randomized pilot study comparing 16 weeks of IPT to brief supportive therapy as treatment for patients with dysthymia suffering from secondary alcohol abuse or dependence. Both treatments were combined with recommendations to attend Alcoholics Anonymous, although few patients did so. The sample size is too small to reveal between-group differences, but each group showed some improvement in depression and reduced alcohol consumption. IPT showed suggestions of greater efficacy in treating depression but no advantage in treating the comorbid alcohol abuse/dependence.

Level of Evidence: (no stars) Negative findings: IPT has been found to be no better than a control condition.

Adaptations

The rationale for using IPT with these patients was the assumption that substance use disorders represent an attempt to compensate for inadequate interpersonal relationships or has a negative consequence on existing relationships. The goal was to help patients resolve interpersonal problems and to develop new skills to alleviate stress and obviate the need for substance use. It was also hoped that patients for whom methadone reduced the craving for opiates would be more likely to engage in psychotherapy.

IPT was used as an adjunctive treatment with methadone-maintained patients and as a sole intervention or combined treatment to achieve abstinence in the treatment of cocaine abusers. Other adaptations to IPT were minor. The content of the sessions was geared to the particular problems of patients with substance abuse, and the focus was switched from treating depression to the reduction or elimination of substance abuse and the development of better social and interpersonal coping strategies.

Patients were encouraged to accept the need to stop drugs, manage impulsivity, and recognize the context of drug use and supply. The interpersonal inventory explored the history of drug use, the family's reaction to it, and the influence of drugs on both the patient's interpersonal behavior and the behaviors necessary to obtain and finance drug use, as well as the illegal behaviors and risks accompanying it. The usual IPT problem areas were used. Since these adaptations have not worked, we cannot recommend that they be used for the treatment of substance abusers.

Many reasons have been suggested for the failure of IPT to show benefit. There were problems in recruiting and retaining patients for the study, and the patients did not seem to believe that the interpersonal focus was relevant to their problems. It was important to stabilize them on methadone in the first study, to relieve their cravings and dysphoria before trying to interest them in psychotherapy. It is also possible that the serious consequences of drug abuse were obviated by the use of sustained methadone maintenance and the accompanying comprehensive drug treatment program, which already included group psychotherapy.

In the dysthymic disorder and alcohol abuse study, IPT therapists focused on achieving sobriety as a role transition. They treated alcohol abuse, like depression, as a medical illness, a condition that was not the patient's fault. Therapists tried to link drinking episodes to interpersonal stresses, both of which patients recorded in a diary. It was usually possible to link both mood shifts and drinking behavior to life circumstances. Patients were also encouraged to attend Alcoholics Anonymous meetings. Participants appear to have shown some gains, but not significantly greater than those seen for other study patients who were randomized to brief supportive psychotherapy.

Comment It has long been clinically acknowledged that substance abuse interferes with many psychotherapeutic approaches. Based on the published literature, it appears that some approaches other than IPT (e.g., cognitive-behavioral therapy) that focus on relapse prevention, motivational interviewing, Alcoholics Anonymous or other 12-step support groups, detoxification, and rehabilitation when appropriate may be preferable for patients with substance use disorders. Once sober, such patients might benefit from IPT techniques to rebuild their lives and relationships, but the benefits of IPT at this point are speculative. IPT has never been intended for all patients with all conditions, and substance abuse may be an area where its application has limited utility.

19

Eating Disorders

Diagnosis

Anorexia nervosa and especially bulimia nervosa are psychiatric syndromes that frequently overlap with mood disorders. Both conditions involve distortions in body image and loss of control over eating behavior (see *DSM-IV*).

IPT was adapted for bulimia by Fairburn and colleagues (Fairburn, Jones, & Peveler, 1991; Fairburn, Jones, Peveler, Hope, & O'Connor, 1993; Fairburn et al., 1995) as an individual therapy and by Wilfley, Mackenzie, Welch, Ayres, & Weissman (2000) and Wilfley et al. (2002) as a group treatment. IPT was slower to take effect than CBT but eventually caught up in two studies of bulimia and was less efficacious than CBT in a third trial (Agras, Walsh, Fairburn, Wilson, & Kraemer, 2000). For anorexia nervosa, a treatment for which no outpatient treatments have shown much benefit, IPT in the only trial conducted showed little benefit as well (McIntosh et al., 2005).

Level of Evidence:

> For individual and group IPT for bulimia nervosa: **** Treatment has been validated by at least two randomized, controlled trials demonstrating the superiority of IPT to a control condition.

> For anorexia nervosa: (no stars) IPT has been found to be no better than a control condition.

Adaptations

Partly because Fairburn wanted to contrast elements of IPT with cognitive behavioral therapy (CBT), he made several changes in IPT for bulimia. First, whereas IPT therapists frequently emphasize that depression is an illness— because depressed patients tend to forget this and blame themselves, confusing themselves with their illness—bulimic patients have no such difficulty. They need no reminders to know they have bulimia and eating difficulties. Therefore, rather than focusing on bulimia as an illness, IPT therapists in Fairburn's studies mentioned the diagnosis at the start of treatment but thereafter avoided discussing food, eating, body image, and so forth—the usual topics of their patients' conversation. Whereas CBT therapists focused on such matters, IPT therapists interrupted their patients when they raised eating topics and steered them back to examining their discomfort with feelings and relationships that might trigger binge episodes. This adjustment to the features of the disorder appeared to be helpful. Thus IPT focused not directly on the eating symptoms, but on their affective and interpersonal context.

Second, because role-playing is also a CBT technique, IPT therapists were asked not to use it in Fairburn's studies. This represents the loss of a potentially powerful aspect of IPT. We do not recommend that IPT therapists avoid role-play in their clinical practice treating bulimia.

The adaptations of IPT as a group treatment for bulimia are described in Chapter 23.

Case Example: Obesity in Her Thoughts

Ms. E, a 27-year-old single assistant editor at a publishing firm, presented with bulimia nervosa. Her chief complaint was "I'm embarrassed to say I can't control my eating."

Ms. E reported repeated a history of bingeing and vomiting since age 14. She tended to eat little, then periodically binged on huge quantities of pound cake or sweets. She was muscular and thin, worked out frequently at the gym, but felt "grossly obese" in ways that "other people can't see" and obsessively checked herself in the mirror for flaws in her figure. Similarly, she weighed herself several times a day and forced herself to vomit if her weight was unacceptable. She threw up at least once a day, a pattern she saw as a necessary ritual. She had social contacts but confided in no one because she was sure that they would be "grossed out" by her eating behavior or turned off by her mood. She kept a similar distance from her family and her roommate. She had had numerous sexual liaisons but declared with negative bravado that she had never had more than three dates with a man. She felt men were "for some reason" attracted to her but that they quickly figured out her ugly side.

Ms. E had shown little benefit from two adequate trials of serotonin reuptake inhibitors, which she felt caused weight gain. She had undergone two courses of psychodynamic psychotherapy, each lasting about 2 years, with little benefit. She presented with worsening bulimia in the wake of "being dumped" by an Internet date and increased pressure at work. Symptoms included worsening binges, a 3-pound weight gain, and subsequently increased purging and exercise. She also reported moderate depressive symptoms (Hamilton Rating Scale for Depression score = 18).

The therapist gave Ms. E the diagnosis of bulimia nervosa. He noted that her eating behavior might be related to her life situation and wondered whether she might be curious about this connection. Picking up on her concern about relationships, he suggested that they spend the next 16 weeks working on understanding the connection between her interpersonal functioning and her symptoms and on building new interpersonal skills. He described this as a role transition in the wake of her latest breakup of a relationship. She agreed.

Although Ms. E often drifted into the topic of food, the therapist would seek the context of her concern: If she had binged, how had she been feeling at that time? Had something happened, or was she anxious about something that was about to occur? What were her feelings? The therapist worked hard to normalize those feelings, which the patient tended to regard as "weird" or abnormal. Once she had begun to acknowledge disappointment and anger and to recognize patterns of these feelings arising in interpersonal contexts, they began to explore options for putting them into words and expressing them to other people:

> *What might you say? . . . How did that sound? Is that saying what you want to say? How comfortable are you in saying "No"?*

Ms. E had difficulties in asserting herself at work and on dates and in setting limits with other people. In her effort to please, she frequently ignored her own wishes, with predictably unhappy results. After a date in which she had felt pawed or a work assignment had been dumped upon her, she frequently felt helpless, a feeling that almost inevitably led to a briefly soothing but soon distressing binge and then to vomiting, which made her feel like a "disgusting freak." She began tentatively to express her feelings, first by defining her hours and job responsibilities with her work colleagues, which relieved some deadline pressures, and then by taking the seemingly riskier step of telling dates what she wanted and did not like on their dates. Initially skeptical that expressing her feelings would do any good, she was surprised by successes in both settings and noted that her eating and mood symptoms had both decreased.

By the end of the 16-week treatment, Ms. E was infrequently bingeing and had not vomited in 4 weeks. Her Ham-D score had returned to the normal range. Moreover, she recognized for the first time the important connection between her interpersonal life and her bulimic symptoms. The therapist congratulated her on her gains, and they agreed to a once-a-month maintenance treatment, during which she has remained almost asymptomatic for 2½ years. Ms. E is now in a sustained relationship for the first time and engaged to be married.

Comment Whether or not associated with comorbid depression, bulimia is treatable with IPT. Ms. E not only mastered her eating symptoms but also did so through grappling with the perhaps still more important arena of her interpersonal life. Like many bulimic patients, Ms. E's obsession with her eating had obscured for her its connection with her feelings and relationships.

20

Anxiety Disorders

Background

The psychotherapeutic treatment of anxiety disorders has been best established for cognitive and behavioral therapies. Some of the *DSM-IV* diagnostic criteria resonate with cognitive thinking, and research has shown that forms of CBT are frequently beneficial for a spectrum of anxiety disorders. Yet not all patients respond to any treatment modality, and while some patients are able to work within the CBT framework, others have trouble accepting it. In recent years, IPT researchers have begun to approach anxiety disorders, including social anxiety disorder (also known as social phobia), posttraumatic stress disorder (PTSD), and panic disorder. Since many anxiety disorders are comorbid with major depression, it would be reassuring for IPT therapists focusing on the latter to know whether it benefits the former diagnoses.

> Level of Evidence: (The evidence varies by disorder; in general, research is in an early stage): ** Encouraging findings in one or more open trials or in pilot studies with small samples. A large-scale trial of IPT for social anxiety disorder is currently under way in Germany.

Adaptations

Anxiety and depression frequently overlap, and the focal IPT problem areas seem to apply to both. Similarly, anxious patients are often inhibited in expressing anger, confronting people, and asserting themselves. At least several of the *DSM* anxiety disorders have important interpersonal aspects. Thus the general IPT approach seems to need little overhaul for anxiety disorders.

Social Anxiety Disorder (Social Phobia)

Like dysthymic disorder (Chapter 16), social anxiety disorder is a chronic syndrome. Individuals with social anxiety disorder fear humiliation in social situations: saying or doing the wrong thing, blushing, or otherwise looking foolish or incompetent in the eyes of others. As a result, they avoid social interactions and close relationships and tend to have few social supports. Thus the central pathology of social phobia seems an appropriate target for IPT.

Because social phobia is a chronic syndrome, Lipsitz, Fyer, Markowitz, & Cherry (1999) applied the idea of an *iatrogenic role transition* to social phobia in the same way that it has been used with dysthymic patients. By exploring new interpersonal options, patients alter maladaptive social inter-actions, function more effectively, and feel better. As they do, they begin to recognize that the long-standing pattern was a treatable illness rather than an integral aspect of themselves. Treatment itself thus becomes a therapist- and patient-initiated role transition to health. Lipsitz and Markowitz (2006) have also substituted the more benign term "role insecurity" as an alternative title to the formulation of "interpersonal deficits" for highly isolated socially anxious patients.

Like dysthymic patients, patients with social phobia have been chronically demoralized about their social functioning and need considerable encouragement, support, and role-playing to enter new social situations. In general, however, the usual IPT approach for depression seems helpful for these patients as well.

A research group in Norway has completed a study testing group IPT and CBT as a treatment for patients with social anxiety disorder and found both treatments equally efficacious (Hoffart, 2005).

Case Example: Scared to Talk

Mr. H, a 35-year-old single businessman, presented for treatment with a life-long history of social anxiety that emerged most dramatically in public speaking situations. Mr. H had grown up with a stutter that he conquered with speech lessons and great effort. Schoolmates had made fun of his speech, and a teacher had once humiliated him in junior high school during a class presentation. To his credit, he had joined his college debate team and felt he had mastered this important area of his life.

Having joined a business firm that required presentations in front of large groups of colleagues and customers, he was then appalled when, in the setting of his father's illness and a romantic disappointment, he blanked, froze, and then completely fell apart with panic symptoms during an important pitch. He subsequently felt intimidated at meetings, worried about blushing, sweating, or having his voice break when talking, and generally retreated from what had been an active and successfully developing career. He felt particularly intimidated by his superior, whom he felt had always been critical of him before, and more so since this incident. This had been a problem for months.

Mr. H had always been "shy," always tentative about relationships outside his family of origin. He was close to his parents and his older sister but had few close friends. Dating was torture: He became so anxious in the presence of the other sex that he could barely speak. He stammered, sweated, blushed, and retreated. He had finally begun a tentative relationship with a coworker some months before the big presentation but felt frightened by her responsiveness and pulled back, then felt humiliated when she subsequently snubbed him.

Mr. H's IPT therapist diagnosed him as having social anxiety disorder with both generalized and specific (public speaking) features. He defined this as a chronic illness that was treatable, not H's fault, and related to his interpersonal discomfort in social situations. Treatment was formulated as a role dispute with his boss, although they acknowledged that his dating breakup was also a treatment issue. They agreed to a 16-week treatment.

Therapy focused on Mr. H's feelings at work and how his interpersonal behavior might communicate or miscommunicate his wishes and needs. He initially discussed talking with coworkers and having lunch with Mike, a colleague whom he liked but who he feared disliked him. Mr. H was uncertain about approaching Mike but agreed with his therapist that it was okay in principle to ask him to have lunch. The therapist validated his wish to have friends, discussed the importance of having social supports, and role-played his saying, "Hey, wanna grab something to eat?" They fine-tuned his words and tone of voice until he was able to do this.

Lunch was planned and went well, as Mr. H admitted even while relating his indigestion afterward. Further social successes with coworkers made him increasingly comfortable and less worried about blushes and stammers. With this gain in confidence, he was willing to address the still-uncomfortable dispute with his boss, Rod. On careful analysis, it appeared that Mr. H was reacting more strongly than might have been warranted to the behavior of his superior, a domineering type who gave little quarter to anyone.

The therapist and Mr. H talked about whether he should take Rod's criticism personally. They again discussed what he wanted from the situation and what options he had to achieve this. Mr. H decided to arrange a meeting to talk over how he was doing and even—with some trepidation— the debacle of his presentation. He approached this meeting sweating, tremulous, and anxious but was able to tell Rod how important his job was to him and that he hoped he had not damaged his chances with the presentation flub. As Mr. H and his therapist had discussed, Rod actually saw the event as far less serious than Mr. H had. What felt like an eternity of silence to Mr. H had only seemed a long pause to him. Rod gruffly told him his future chances were "as good as anyone's."

This was a great relief to Mr. H. His symptoms continued to recede, but he remained nervous about making public presentations. When, near the end of treatment, the opportunity arose to give another pitch, he was quite nervous. He and his therapist discussed and role-played contingencies, including what he would say if (when) he felt uneasy giving his talk. Anxiety symptoms were described as such, rather than some personal defect. The talk went fairly well: Mr. H was nervous but got through it.

At the end of 16 weeks Mr. H's social anxiety disorder was under good control. He and his therapist then contracted for a year of monthly maintenance therapy, during which he continued to do well at work, made several successful big presentations, and began to work on dating, too.

Comment For many patients, the structure of a work role, with its built-in job description, makes it easier to address than the uncharted dangers of social life. Once patients have gained confidence in the work arena, they may feel willing to risk the social scene. Mr. H provides an illustration of this.

Posttraumatic Stress Disorder

Psychotherapies for PTSD have almost invariably focused on exposure to memories or concrete reminders of past traumas. Some patients refuse or cannot tolerate this approach. As is the case for major depression, it may be helpful to have several effective psychotherapeutic approaches to PTSD. Accordingly, Bleiberg and Markowitz (2005) tested IPT as a treatment for patients with chronic PTSD that is not based on their exposure. This treatment noted that trauma had led the patients to mistrust and retreat from their social environment. IPT focused not on patients' confronting trauma directly but on how they handled their daily social interactions—expressing their feelings to and setting limits with other people. Although therapists did not ask patients to expose themselves to traumatic reminders, as they improved they frequently did so spontaneously. IPT is also appropriate for treating the comorbid depression many patients with PTSD describe.

Case Example: Mugged in the Subway

Mr. A, a 37-year-old industrial worker, had been robbed at knifepoint by a teenager in his neighborhood subway station 2 years before. He was horrified that he had nearly died for a few dollars and had repeated flashbacks and nightmares about the event. He began to avoid subways and buses and instead walked quite a distance to and from work. He retreated from friends, coworkers, and his wife of 12 years, feeling he could not trust anything and that his world was shattered. He also felt ashamed of having been robbed by a "kid" and hid this humiliating story from others. His symptoms included insomnia, anxious and depressed mood, a pronounced startle reaction, and a sense that his life was over. On presentation to treatment, he met *DSM-IV* criteria for both PTSD and major depressive disorder.

The IPT therapist sympathized with what Mr. A had been through, gave him the diagnoses of PTSD and MDD, as well as the sick role, and defined the event as a role transition. In recounting what had been lost, Mr. A focused on his formerly close relationship with his wife. He now hid out from her in the bedroom. He also restricted her activities outside the house as he feared that she, too, would be attacked. Their sexual relationship had ended with the mugging, and he no longer felt he could be close to or confide in her. Similarly, he had retreated from his coworkers.

Therapist and patient agreed that the aftershock of the mugging on Mr. A's social functioning was "adding insult to injury." The therapist noted Mr. A's former interpersonal strengths and the loss of social supports following his attack. They discussed how he could "reclaim his life" and particularly his marriage. After discussion and role-playing, he went home and had the most open discussion with Mrs. A in years. He apologized to her for ruining their marriage and their lives. To his surprise, she was sympathetic, did not regard him as a weakling, and asked how they could make things better. He returned the next week to treatment feeling considerably better.

The couple's relationship continued to improve, and their sex life resumed. Emboldened, he began to risk fraternizing more with his coworkers. By the ninth of 14 sessions, both his PTSD and MDD had remitted. In the termination phase, Mr. A confided that he had resumed taking public transportation, including the subway, although this was not an issue on which therapy had focused. He remained asymptomatic at a 6-month follow-up.

Note that treatment did not focus on exposure or on symptoms such as flashbacks, but rather on interpersonal interactions and the rebuilding of social supports. By focusing on this one arena, IPT seems to produce benefits that generalize to yield overall improvement and are not limited to the interpersonal area.

Krupnick (1999) at Georgetown University have conducted a randomized controlled trial comparing group IPT to treatment as usual with low-income women with chronic PTSD recruited from public gynecology clinics. Results were apparently quite positive. In Australia, Robertson, Rushton, Bartrum, & Ray (2004) have also described a group IPT approach to PTSD, although this has not been systematically tested.

Panic Disorder

Lipsitz, Gur, Miller, Vermes, & Fyer (2006) have also conducted a small pilot open trial of IPT for panic disorder, again finding marked improvement in most of the patients they treated. This trial applied the standard IPT approach for depression to panic disorder. They focused on pervasive, more prolonged interpersonal problems associated with onset and maintenance of panic disorder. Most of the patients fit formulations for either role transition or role dispute.

Comment All of the findings for IPT in anxiety disorders are encouraging but preliminary and need confirmation in controlled trials. The general IPT approach for mood disorders seems translatable to these anxiety disorders with little adaptation of the IPT approach. It is noteworthy that social phobia, PTSD, and panic disorder all contain strong interpersonal elements. IPT might be expected to be harder to apply to, and less effective for, a more internalized disorder such as obsessive-compulsive disorder.

21

Borderline Personality Disorder

Diagnosis

IPT has generally targeted Axis I and explicitly *not* Axis II disorders. Its brief time frame and attention to relatively acute symptoms lend itself to this Axis I focus. Yet extension of IPT to Axis I syndromes such as dysthymic disorder and social anxiety disorder suggests that IPT might benefit more chronically ill psychiatric patients. Indeed, social anxiety disorder overlaps significantly with avoidant personality disorder. Can IPT treat personality disorders?

Borderline personality disorder (BPD) is a prevalent, debilitating syndrome. Patients with BPD are high users of mental health services and have historically been associated with a poor prognosis. This disorder is closely associated with mood disorders; indeed, mood instability is a key dimension of the syndrome. Other features of BPD are identity diffusion, cognitive distortions, and, of interest to IPT therapists, interpersonal impairment. BPD is associated with high rates of suicidal ideation, parasuicidal gestures, and completed suicide.

In recent years, research has indicated that treatments as diverse as dialectical behavioral therapy (DBT; Linehan, Armstrong, Suárez, Allmon, & Heard, 1991) and a psychodynamic approach to day hospital (Bateman and Fonagy, 2001) can effectively treat patients with BPD. Further, careful longitudinal studies have demonstrated that this diagnosis, once considered nearly hopeless, may remit over time with or perhaps even without treatment (Shea et al., 2002).

Level of Evidence: * Under testing

Adaptation

Tentative consideration of the application of IPT to Axis II has appeared. In a small, unpublished trial partly confounded by medication use, Angus and Gillies (1994) felt that 12 weekly sessions of IPT held promise as a treatment for patients with BPD. Markowitz, Skodol, and Bleiberg (2006) at Columbia are currently conducting an open trial of an 8-month adaptation of IPT for patients with borderline personality disorder who are in interpersonal crisis. Their initial impression is that BPD overlaps meaningfully with mood disorder and produces a host of interpersonal difficulties.

The Columbia adaptation involves changes in standard IPT relating to (1) the conceptualization and (2) chronicity of the disorder, (3) difficulties in forming and maintaining the treatment alliance, (4) length of treatment, (5) suicide risk, (6) termination, and (7) choice of subjects within the BPD spectrum of diagnosis (Markowitz, 2005; Markowitz, Skodol, & Bleiberg, 2006). The value of these adaptations and of IPT as a treatment for borderline personality disorder will depend on the outcome of such studies.

Conceptualization

Borderline personality disorder is presented to the patient as a poorly named syndrome that has a significant depressive component. A major difference between MDD and BPD is that, while depressed patients often have difficulty expressing any anger, patients with BPD often do the same much of the time but then periodically explode with excessive anger, which reinforces their tendency to avoid expressing anger whenever possible. The goals of treatment are, as is usually the case in IPT, to link mood (including anger) to interpersonal situations, to find better ways of handling such situations, and to build better social supports and skills. Psychoeducation about BPD includes clarification of the current versus the historical meanings of the diagnosis.

The chronicity of the BPD diagnosis links it to IPT approaches for both dysthymic disorder and social phobia, in which long-standing behavioral patterns become associated with one's sense of self. By defining such patterns as part of the illness rather than part of the person, the therapist can help to make them ego alien and help the patient to change.

The treatment alliance is somewhat more fragile and complex in working with patients with BPD than in those with MDD. Whereas IPT typically avoids a direct focus on therapist-patient interactions, this becomes unavoidable when problems arise in the alliance. When such problems crop up, the therapist addresses them in a here-and-now, interpersonal fashion, rather than making psychodynamic interpretations (see the case example below).

Treatment has been conceptualized as having two phases: first, 18 sessions in 16 weeks, with a focus on building a strong treatment alliance, providing a formulation, and introducing IPT concepts. Assuming this initial phase goes well, the second phase comprises 16 additional sessions in as many weeks, or a total of 8 months of more or less weekly psychotherapy. In addition, therapists may check in with patients for once-a-week, 10-minute telephone checks.

Self-destructive behavior and suicide risk are concerns for BPD as for MDD. Close monitoring of suicidality is warranted with such patients. Suicidal behavior has not been a frequent problem in the trial thus far.

Because patients with BPD are extremely sensitive to abandonment, termination is discussed early and often in the treatment. Using this approach, termination has been sad but successful for these patients, who have generally found treatment helpful.

Because it seemed important to work on ongoing maladaptive interpersonal behavioral patterns, this initial IPT trial has enrolled patients with *DSM-IV* BPD who have interpersonal crises of one sort or another, excluding extremely isolated (interpersonal deficits) patients with comorbid schizotypal or schizoid personality disorders.

Case Example: Beyond the Rage

Mr. A, a 38-year-old unemployed man, presented with BPD and paranoid personality disorder. He described a long history of alcohol dependence but was now sober. His principal affect was rage, and he had run through seven sponsors in Alcoholics Anonymous. Despite the therapist's attempts to focus on his daily life outside the therapy office, Mr. A's hypersensitivity to his interaction with the therapist led to frequent disruptions. He noticed and objected if the tape recorder had been moved a few inches from one session to the next. He objected to the therapist's jewelry and stylish clothing. Once angered, he would storm out of the office, slamming the door and announcing he would not return. Yet return he did—to repeat the scenario.

The therapist, despite doubts about whether treatment could proceed, persevered. She noted that anger was the problem that had brought Mr. A to treatment and that it was a key symptom of BPD. It was just what they needed to work on. She apologized for upsetting the patient and explored his options for expressing his feelings about relationships. Note that the therapeutic alliance was addressed in interpersonal terms in the here and now, not with psychodynamic interpretations. As soon as things were mended in the office, the therapist tried to focus on anger difficulties in outside relationships: at AA, in his neighborhood, and in potential job leads. Although the angry pattern continued, it changed over time. With the therapist's tolerance and support, the patient began to stay longer in sessions where he felt enraged, at first fuming silently. Later in treatment, he was able not only to remain in the room but also to voice his feelings. The treatment focus then shifted back to outside relationships. He began to discuss his related fears of abandonment and of dropping his guard lest others reject him.

Once the therapeutic alliance had been stabilized, the focus on outside relationships began in earnest. Mr. A continued to have difficulties with his AA sponsor. He was devoted to him but also felt as though his sponsor had frequently betrayed him. The therapist was able to validate some of his anger and help Mr. A choose more muted expressions of it in role-playing. Encounters with the sponsor were successful, and that relationship was maintained, whereas previous sponsorships had failed. By the end of the 8-month therapy Mr. A was more active in AA, friendlier with friends there and in his neighborhood, and seemed on the verge of getting a job after 2 years of unemployment. He no longer met criteria for BPD and was far less depressed. He was even able to haltingly tell his therapist he had learned a lot in treatment and would miss her. (This case example has been adapted, with the publisher's permission, from Markowitz, Skodol, and Bleiberg, 2006.)

Section IV

Special Topics, Training, and Resources

22

IPT Across Cultures and in Developing Countries

Overview

IPT has been used successfully in a variety of cultures, both within and outside the United States. IPT training programs have been conducted in Australia, Austria, Brazil, China, the Czech Republic, Ethiopia, Finland, France, Germany, Greece, Hungary, Iceland, India, Ireland, Italy, Japan, the Netherlands, New Zealand, Norway, Romania, Spain, Sweden, Switzerland, Thailand, Turkey, Uganda, and the United Kingdom. Versions of the IPT manual have been translated into Italian, Japanese, German, and French). The International Society for Interpersonal Psychotherapy has a website (http://www.interpersonalpsychotherapy.org/) and holds meetings that bring clinicians and researchers together from all over the world.

In the United States, IPT has been used successfully in clinical trials with patients from African American and Hispanic (mainly Puerto Rican and Dominican) backgrounds. Yet to date, little systematic work has been devoted to examining differences in the way IPT is practiced in treating patients from these varied cultural environments. Furthermore, adaptations have focused on the treatment of major depressive disorder. The only nonmood adaptation of IPT to date in a non-Anglo culture is a Norwegian group treatment for patients with social phobia in a residential setting (Hoffart, 2005).

Principles of Cultural Adaptation

The principles of adapting IPT to cultural issues are simple, although their implementation may pose important challenges for the clinician and the patient. It is imperative that IPT clinicians proceed carefully in discussing cultures they do not belong to. We have included some guidelines here:

1. A person familiar with the culture must be a member of the team assisting in any adaptation.

2. It is essential to understand how the symptoms of the disorder being treated present clinically and are interpreted in the culture.
3. It is crucial to know what interventions will be acceptable in the patient's culture. Those that are deemed appropriate in mainstream American culture may be seen as insensitive or disrespectful in other cultures.
4. It is useful to differentiate between the problem areas (grief, disputes, etc.) of IPT, which may be universal triggers for depression, and the techniques used to achieve change or resolution, which are culturally bound.

The cultural context of the problem areas also requires understanding. For example, marital disputes may arise in the context of marital infidelity, which has a different meaning in the context of a culture where marriage is uncommon or where more than one wife is the norm. The range of acceptable responses to this situation may similarly differ across cultures. Yet the emotional issues in a marital dispute of betrayal, fear of abandonment, and concern about economic security for oneself and one's children may be the same throughout these cultural contexts. The development of depression in association with disputes, as well as the nature of these disputes, whether at an impasse, in negotiation, or in dissolution, also may not differ by culture. Culturally appropriate options for resolving disputes (i.e., the strategies used for achieving resolution) must be recognized and respected (e.g., expressing opinions verbally and directly in parts of the United States; actions such as cooking a bad meal in Uganda; or gaining the support of relatives in some Latino cultures).

The ease of translating IPT for depression into diverse cultures probably reflects the fact that the problem areas identified in IPT as triggers of depression (e.g., death of a loved one, disagreements with important persons in one's life, life changes that disrupt close attachments) are intrinsic, universal elements of the human condition that transcend culture. The experience of using IPT in diverse cultures suggests that these triggers of depression and disruptions of human attachment are conserved across cultures (Miller, 2006).

> Level of Evidence: **** The evidence is excellent that IPT for major depressive disorders is efficacious in different cultures. However, the substantiation for each culture is based upon only one or two trials. The support for the cross-cultural translation of IPT consists of a clinical trial in Uganda (Bolton et al., 2003), trials of Hispanic youth in Puerto Rico and the continental United States (e.g., Rossello & Bernal, 1999, Mufson, Pollack Dorta, Wickramaratne, et al., 2004), and trials outside the United States (e.g., Blom, Hoencamp, & Zwaan, 1996; Feijò de Mello et al., 2001). In 2006 Paula Ravitz, a medical doctor, spent a month teaching IPT at Addis Ababa University in Ethiopia.

We present our experience in modifying IPT and testing it in a developing country as an experience that may be relevant to much cross-cultural treatment, and we also present Ravitz's description of her Ethiopian training since she used the Ugandan study as a model.

The Ugandan Experience

Epidemiological studies conducted in the past quarter century have indicated a substantial level of depression in Uganda and a current prevalence of about 21% (Bolton et al., 2003). Local people considered depression a consequence of the HIV epidemic in Uganda, which has one of the highest rates of HIV infection in the world. Many traditional healers in these communities, interviewed during a 2000 survey, expressed their inability to treat depression using local methods. The dearth and high cost of physicians and medication preempted the use of antidepressants, especially in rural areas. Psychotherapy was seen as a viable treatment option so long as there was evidence of its effectiveness. However, psychotherapy could not require highly trained mental health providers, due to their scarcity, and had to be conducted in groups to increase coverage and reduce cost.

IPT was selected because it had an evidence base for depression, because it could be administered in a group format, and because Bolton, the clinician directing the work, was familiar with Uganda and felt that IPT was compatible with a culture in which people consider themselves as part of a family and a community before they see themselves as individuals. Interpersonal relations are extremely important in Uganda.

The adaptation of IPT for Uganda retained the basic structure of IPT but simplified it for use by nonclinicians (Clougherty, Verdeli, & Weissman, 2003). The simplification resembles IPC (described in Chapter 15), but this was group, not individual, treatment. The interpersonal foci were detailed in scripts written in plain language. Grief was called the "death of a loved one." Role disputes were termed "disagreements," and transitions became "life changes." Interpersonal deficits translated to "loneliness and shyness," but this category was dropped during the training since the local workers felt it irrelevant to their culture. Since all of life takes place in groups, people are never alone. This situation might not apply in many other communities. Modifications to improve cultural relevance were made on site, based on information from the trainee group leaders, who had grown up and lived in the participating districts and were college-educated, non–mental health workers. Training was conducted in English by two U.S. IPT experts assisted by two mental health professionals who had lived and worked in the area.

Basic Group Structure

Assigned to each group were 8–10 persons 18 years of age and older with major depression. Men and women attended separate groups as the leader felt that patients would not talk freely in a coed group. Two individual and

16 weekly group sessions of 90 minutes each were conducted by a trained leader. There were four treatment phases including:

1. Two pregroup individual sessions, in which the leader learned the patient's symptoms, made diagnoses, explained depression as a medical illness, and began to formulate the individual's interpersonal problems associated with the onset of the symptoms. Leaders used the standard IPT first phase of IPT treatment (see Chapter 2), elicited information about triggers of the depressive episode, and determined one or two problem areas to work on. The leader individually explained how the group would work:

   Everyone in the group will be asked to talk about the problems that brought out their depression, listen to the problems of others, and find new ways of understanding and handling these problems in order to feel less depressed.

   The leader then detailed the frequency and length of meetings and received confirmation that the person would like to join the group.

2. Beginning group (4 sessions): The group members learned each other's symptoms and problems, and the leader explained how the group would work. Participants were told that the group was a place to learn and practice skills that would help them manage interpersonal problems that had led to their depression. During the sessions, group members were encouraged to talk about their depressive symptoms and the social situations that worsened the depression or brought it about; to listen to and help each other; to suggest ways of handling problems; and to practice new ways of coping.

3. Working (10 sessions): In the middle phase, the members discussed their problems and feelings and tried to make changes in their lives.

4. Ending (2 sessions): These group sessions involved a summary of changes in symptoms and problems and discussion of possible new problems that might bring about depression. Time was allotted to express feelings about ending the group and to explore how the participants could continue to help one another.

The process did not differ from that used in group IPT conducted in the United States (see Chapter 23). We considered the treatment IPC because the group therapists were not mental health workers, and we wrote out the scripts to guide them. The leader was not judgmental or condemning and discussed confidentiality with group members. Because of the experience the developing countries had had with nongovernment organizations (NGOs), it was important in the initial phase to clarify that group leaders were not providing patients with material goods.

The Ugandan trainees were familiar with the state of depression but had their own words to describe it (Verdeli et al., 2003). These terms were compatible with common depressive signs and symptoms such as sadness, poor sleep and appetite, self-neglect, suicidality, jitteriness, low energy, and feelings of worthlessness. Regarding confidentiality, group members were asked not to disclose the content of the group meetings to people outside the group. However, this secrecy risked being misconstrued as conspiracy, perhaps suggesting that the village was starting a new political movement or encouraging women to use birth control. Therefore, the leader encouraged group members to generally describe the group's purpose to the community and to relatives but to avoid discussion of specific content. Meetings were held in community centers, churches, and open spaces as available. In order to accommodate community events such as funerals or weddings, in which the whole village participated, scheduling was flexible. Interruptions (e.g., relatives of group members wanting to talk to someone, breast-feeding children crying for their mothers) were expected.

The problem areas fit well with the reality of the problems experienced by the Ugandan community. Grief was associated with the death of a family member or close friend, often due to AIDS. Because of cultural intolerance of any negative mention of the dead, evinced in the popular saying, "The dead are living among us," the closest formulation of a question aimed at capturing negative experiences with the deceased was "Were there times in your life together when you felt disappointed?"

Disagreements were arguments with neighbors about property boundaries or stolen animals; political fights; family members claiming privileges that traditionally belonged to other members; wives protesting the husband's bringing in of a second wife or acceding—out of fear—to an HIV-affected husband's demand not to use condoms. The issue here was how to get one's point across without necessarily being direct. Whereas Westerners might state their expectation of another person directly, in Uganda such directness would be perceived as inappropriate and disrespectful.

For example, a woman who was angry at her husband could not discuss her concerns with him directly but could start cooking bad food, which would be a signal to him that something was wrong. An indirect way of addressing disagreements was to engage relatives in resolving disputes between two parties or to encourage a woman to discuss the prospects of her children becoming orphans rather than invoking her own health when pleading with an HIV-infected man to use protection. If that failed to work, she could enlist the help of a medical person or a traditional healer whom the husband could trust without suspicion that another man was seducing his wife.

Another challenge involved finding culturally appropriate options for resolving a dispute. For example, when discussing the options available to an infertile woman, the trainees responded that she should ask her sister or another woman to marry her husband, so that the new wife would be an ally and they could raise the children together.

Life changes (i.e., role transitions) included becoming sick with AIDS and other illnesses, unemployment, marriage and moving to the husband's house, and dealing with the husband's decision to marry a new wife, which inevitably altered the first wife's position in the household. In working on a role transition in standard IPT, the therapist helps the patient to recognize positive and negative aspects of the old and the new roles. For many of the experiences in Uganda—the devastation of war, tyrannical regimes, torture, AIDS, and hunger—finding positive aspects of the life change was difficult. Instead, the trainees identified and focused on elements that were under the individuals' control and worked on building skills and identifying options such as persuading potential advocates for assistance.

Acceptance of the approach was high. Attendance was excellent, and dropout from the groups was low (7.8%). There was impressive evidence of efficacy (Bolton et al., 2003). The groups actually continued to meet on their own after the official termination.

The themes that reflected the culture were the centrality of the extended family, (including multiple wives) as well as the extended community (the village), the avoidance of direct confrontation, which could lead to unforgivable statements and the loss of the relationship. These themes are present in many cultures. Given the considerable cultural differences between Uganda and the United States, the researchers found that the adaptations that were required to translate IPT from one place to another were surprisingly minor and the predicaments of depressed individuals continents apart were quite similar. In many other cultures, IPT is likely to need far less adjustment. Dutch clinicians who initially saw IPT as an overly optimistic, American can-do therapy that would not work under the cloudy Netherlands skies were impressed by its efficacy in their own hands. IPT apparently required little adaptation in Holland or Puerto Rico. These positive experiences are presented against the need for the therapist's familiarity with the culture.

The Ethiopian Experience

The Toronto Addis Ababa Psychiatric Project (TAAPP) was established in 2003 as an educational collaboration between Addis Ababa University and the University of Toronto, Faculty of Medicine, Department of Psychiatry, to develop psychiatric residency training in Ethiopia. Prior to the setting up of this postgraduate training program, Ethiopian psychiatrists were trained only outside of the country. The clinical needs there are great in view of the fact that only 11 psychiatrists were serving a population of more than 70 million. In 2006, an additional 7 psychiatrists, the first Ethiopian trained, joined the ranks. Paula Ravitz, a medical doctor, conducted the IPT-TAAPP, which was a month-long, intensive, interactive, didactic, and clinically contextualized course for psychiatry residents in Interpersonal Psychotherapy.

The course focused on skills acquisition and IPT principles. The curriculum was delivered through readings, workshops, didactic, and bedside teaching with the residents in their clinical settings. These included ward rounds with case discussions, observed interviews, and inpatient group therapy. A key task was to culturally and structurally adapt IPT to the Ethiopian context. The curriculum examined the clinical presentation and epidemiology of depression in Ethiopia (Kedebe & Alem, 1999), the nature of associated life stressors in Ethiopia (Alem, Destal, & Araya, 1995), along with cultural perspectives and case formulation in psychotherapy (Lo & Fung, 2003). Large group teaching included literature reviews and didactic lectures interwoven with case material and role-plays derived from Ethiopian clinical psychiatric practice settings, which served to integrate principles in practice. To facilitate the transfer of knowledge to practice and to further reinforce learning, laminated pocket cards summarizing IPT practice principles were created that trainees could use as quick reminders.

Adaptations

The content- and phase-specific IPT tasks are easily applied to many psychiatric illnesses in this context. IPT provides helpful clinical guidelines to assist in assessment and case formulation of patients in the acute treatment phase; help patients to resolve interpersonal crises in both inpatient and outpatient treatment settings; and facilitate more effective discharge planning, including contingency and aftercare considerations.

Universal experiences related to the IPT problem areas of loss, change, and disagreements were evident in almost every patient. Affectively charged and chronologically linked with the onset or worsening of symptoms, these included postpartum stresses, divorce, loss of loved ones, loss of functional capacity due to infectious diseases (including HIV), forced migration, job loss, and civil unrest. The patients Ravitz saw in Addis Ababa presented in the context of numerous adverse life events of relevance to the application of IPT in this setting.

Less frequent (i.e., less than weekly) or shorter (i.e., less than an hour) sessions were found more feasible. Somatic presentations of psychiatric illness were common in Ethiopia and needed to be addressed. Also relevant was a sensitive awareness of ethnic diversity that is at times politicized. Different ethnic groups have different languages, as well as varied cultural, religious, and social practices. It was essential not to make assumptions about what is culturally accepted in terms of social practices. Similar to the Ugandan context, indirect communication is often used and could be effective; thus therapists had to be open to exploring this option when conducting communication and decisional analyses with patients.

Ravitz concluded that they established the clinical relevance and feasibility of IPT in Ethiopia as an effective therapeutic adjunct with a diverse group of psychiatric patients. To determine whether knowledge translation and dissemination efforts (such as this project) lead to sustained changes in practice and improved patient outcomes, further research is needed. Moreover, outcome research is called for to examine IPT adaptations for settings that present high service demands and cultural diversity.

23

Group, Conjoint, and Telephone Formats for IPT

IPT was developed as an individual psychotherapy, but its principles may be flexibly applied in other formats. This section briefly describes group, conjoint, and telephone adaptations of IPT. Throughout the book, examples of these adaptations are presented.

Group IPT

Group therapy has several evident advantages for IPT. It reduces interpersonal isolation by providing an environment in which to discuss and resolve interpersonal problems. It allows patients to see that others share their illness, validating the IPT sick role. Patients may also feel gratified to find that they are able to help other group members. Group psychotherapy also allows a therapist to treat larger numbers of patients, making it a potentially cost-effective alternative or a more viable treatment in situations in which resources are limited.

Group therapy has potential disadvantages as well. Patients receive less individual attention from the IPT therapist. Moreover, difficulties in assembling adequate numbers of patients to form a group may lead to treatment delay. More specific to IPT, group therapy raises the risk of confusion if patients present with different focal interpersonal problem areas. Inasmuch as a strength of IPT is the precision of its focus, group IPT risks diminishing that organizing clarity.

Wilfley and colleagues (1993) developed the first group IPT adaptation in a study of nonpurging bulimic patients (Chapter 19). The approach combined two initial individual sessions with subsequent group sessions. The individual visits allowed the therapist to develop a therapeutic alliance with each patient and prepare the patient for the group while determining the patient's history, symptoms, and IPT formulation. That constituted the first phase. Once the group began, therapists sent patients home with feedback specific to their own cases.

Wilfley and colleagues (ibid.) addressed the issue of contrary IPT foci by giving all of the patients the formulation of interpersonal deficits. This is interesting: In depression, the term "interpersonal deficits" implies social isolation and difficulties in group interactions. The term clearly meant something different for bulimic patients in view of the fact that they could interact at a superficial level in group but had difficulty in revealing intimate feelings. The shared interpersonal formulation provided a helpful homogeneity to the group, just as the shared diagnosis of bulimia did.

With these changes, group IPT functions much like individual IPT. The overall structure of initial, middle, and termination sessions persists. The focus remains on the connection between feelings and life situations, and patients identify common themes and work together to help one another solve their interpersonal problems.

The first adaptation of IPT in a group format for depression was the Ugandan study (see Chapter 22 for a description of the format, phases, and efficacy). It is also being tested for depressed adolescents in the United States (Mufson, Pollack Dorta, Wickramaratne, et al., 2004) (see Chapter 13) and postpartum depression for women on public assistance (Zlotnick et al., 2001). A Norwegian group has completed a 10-week study of IPT for social anxiety disorder in a residential treatment facility (Chapter 20).

In different trials, group treatments have involved two to three participants and 16–20 weekly group sessions of 90 minutes each.

Level of Evidence

**** Treatment has been validated by at least two randomized controlled trials demonstrating the superiority of IPT to a control condition for bulimia.

*** Validated by one randomized trial for depression in Uganda.

As this book goes to press, a second positive clinical trial in Uganda for depressed adolescents has just been submitted for publication (Clougherty personal communication, October 2006).

Recommendations

Therapists undertaking group IPT should have experience with both the group format and the target diagnosis. Efforts should be made to maximize homogeneity: Patients should share a diagnosis (ideally, their interpersonal focus). For example, if group IPT for depression were to be delivered in a residential facility, it might reasonably gather patients struggling with complicated bereavement in one group, those with role disputes in another, and so on.

Conjoint (Couples) IPT

IPT and couples therapy share an interest in interpersonal interactions. Indeed, individual IPT treatment focusing on role disputes often has the feel of a unilateral "couples" therapy, helping the patient to resolve a marital impasse. Only one small pilot study has been conducted of conjoint IPT, which compared it to individual IPT in treating depressed married women (Foley, Rounsaville, Weissman, Sholomskas, & Chevron, 1989). Conjoint and individual IPT showed equal improvement in depressive symptoms, but those in conjoint IPT reported greater marital satisfaction.

An important aspect of conjoint IPT for depression is the need to diagnose both parties. People are generally attracted to individuals like themselves. In the case of couples therapy, both spouses may be depressed. The therapist should interview each partner separately before beginning the conjoint phase of treatment.

Conjoint IPT starts as an individual treatment of the identified patient, with the spouse brought in to assist. Role transitions and especially role disputes are common.

Level of Evidence: ** Encouraging findings in one or more open trials or in pilot studies with small samples (fewer than 12 subjects).

Recommendations

This approach is intuitively appealing, and the one small study that was conducted was encouraging. Nonetheless, this has been a relatively neglected area of IPT research. Therapists using this approach should be familiar with both couples therapy and the target diagnosis.

Telephone IPT

The telephone is a powerful method of communication that has been increasingly used as a vector for psychotherapy. It may provide convenience of access for patients who are homebound, unable to arrange childcare, or live in remote locales far from therapists. Furthermore, some patients may prefer the relative anonymity and distance of a telephone contact. However, the tradeoffs for the therapist are the inability to see the patient's demeanor and facial reactions and the difficulty in intervening if the patient reports feeling suicidal. There is also the potential for loss of confidentiality on an open telephone line. (The same issues apply to psychotherapy conducted over the Internet.)

A few small studies have used telephone IPT as a treatment. In these projects, patients generally reported that they liked the approach, and some even stated that they preferred it to face-to-face contact. The approach, however, is standard IPT. Most treatments begin with an in-person interview to determine the patient's diagnosis and degree of suicidality, after which treatment takes place by telephone.

> Level of Evidence: ** Encouraging findings in open trials or in pilot studies with small samples (fewer than 12 subjects).

Donnelly and colleagues (2000) piloted this approach in treating homebound cancer patients who were too ill to come to sessions (see Chapter 15). Miller and Weissman (2002) used the telephone to treat depressed patients in partial remission. Neugebauer, Kline, Bleiberg, and colleagues (in press) and Neugebauer, Kline, Markowitz, et al. (2006) used the approach to treat patients with subsyndromal depression postmiscarriage (see Chapter 12). Note that all of these trials limited the patients' severity of depressive symptomatology and suicide risk because the therapist was not actually "seeing" the patient.

Recommendations

Therapists should be experienced in IPT and in treatment of the target diagnosis. Patients should be seen in person before beginning therapy to determine their suitability for this "long-distance" treatment. This decision will depend upon clinical judgment, but patients at high risk of impulsivity, violence, or suicide are probably not good candidates for this approach. If the therapist cannot actually see the patient, a proxy visit with a nearby clinician (e.g., a family doctor) might be indicated. Telephone IPT sessions may also be conducted as part of standard IPT if a patient or the therapist leaves town but wishes to maintain momentum in the treatment.

24

Training and Resources

Increasingly, evidence-based psychotherapies like IPT are being offered to patients, and patients are requesting them as information begins to filter into the popular press. Training programs are beginning to incorporate these treatments, although progress is slow (Weissman, Verdeli, et al., 2006; Lichtmacher, Eisendrath, & Haller, 2006). In the meantime, how do you become a skillful IPT practitioner?

The course is relatively easy if you have already had basic training in psychotherapy, including how to listen and talk to patients; express empathy and warmth, hold back your own reactions and opinions; formulate a problem; maintain a therapeutic alliance; understand the limits of confidentiality; and maintain professional boundaries and ethical practice. A basic familiarity with clinical psychiatric diagnosis is essential. Learning IPT is discovering how to take your basic psychotherapy training and modify it for use with a specific set of strategies.

Read the IPT Manual

The version you are reading has been designed to highlight the basic elements and take you through the strategies. An IPT manual that describes these procedures and IPT adaptations more fully is *Comprehensive Guide to Interpersonal Psychotherapy* (Weissman et al., 2000).

Attend an IPT Training Workshop

There are continuing medical educational (CME) courses given at many of the annual meetings of professional organizations. The American Psychiatric Association, for example, has at least two workshops on IPT at its annual meeting. These are usually half- or full-day courses and are primarily didactic. Such courses may reinforce your IPT reading and allow clarifications of questions you may have about IPT.

Some academic centers offer 2- to 4-day workshops that are much more intensive and provide some practical (hands-on) training. These have been held throughout the world, particularly in England, Canada, and New Zealand. Since the sites change, the best way to learn about workshops and supervision is through the International Society of Interpersonal Psychotherapy (http://www.interpersonalpsychotherapy.org/). For a small fee you can become a member and receive its newsletter. Every 2 years an international meeting of IPT is held, where practitioners and researchers from all over the world present their experiences in using IPT.

Obtain Clinical Supervision With an Experienced IPT Clinician

If you are serious about becoming an expert or a trainer in IPT, clinical supervision with an expert IPT clinician is an essential step. Although there is no official certification program, the experts recommend at least two to three supervised cases in IPT completed with an experienced IPT therapist. Supervision is usually weekly, either one-on-one or in small groups, and should use audiotapes or videotapes of actual sessions. Ask patients for written consent to tape their treatment sessions, with the understanding that you will maintain confidentiality and use the tapes only for supervisory purposes and then erase them. Evidence indicates that continuing education or other courses that are simply didactic lectures without interactive supervision do *not* change clinicians' performance (Davis, Thomson O'Brien, Freemantle, et al., 1999). Our own studies show that selected, experienced psychotherapists can competently perform IPT on a high level after as little as one supervised case (Rounsaville, Chevron, Weissman, Prusoff, & Frank, 1986).

If you cannot afford the time and expense of a full program, read the book and attend a workshop; if you can, audiotape a few cases with the patients' permission and have an experienced IPT therapist listen to and critique them. From time to time, training tapes have become available. There are also translations of the IPT manual into Japanese, Italian, French, and German; additional translations are planned. The best way to learn about these is through the International Society of IPT or by writing to the author.

Chapter 22 describes the training of mental health and non–mental health professionals in developing countries.

A list of IPT translations and associated manuals is given separately in the References.

Appendix A

Hamilton Rating Scale for Depression

THE HAMILTON RATING SCALE FOR DEPRESSION

(to be administered by a health care professional)

Patient's Name

Date of Assessment

To rate the severity of depression in patients who are already diagnosed as depressed, administer this questionnaire. The higher the score, the more severe the depression.

For each item, write the correct number on the line next to the item. (Only one response per item)

1. DEPRESSED MOOD (Sadness, hopeless, helpless, worthless)

———

    0= Absent
    1= These feeling states indicated only on questioning
    2= These feeling states spontaneously reported verbally
    3= Communicates feeling states non-verbally—i.e., through facial expression, posture, voice, and tendency to weep
    4= Patient reports VIRTUALLY ONLY these feeling states in his spontaneous verbal and non-verbal communication

2. FEELINGS OF GUILT

———

    0= Absent
    1= Self reproach, feels he has let people down
    2= Ideas of guilt or rumination over past errors or sinful deeds
    3= Present illness is a punishment. Delusions of guilt
    4= Hears accusatory or denunciatory voices and/or experiences threatening visual hallucinations

3. SUICIDE

———

    0= Absent
    1= Feels life is not worth living
    2= Wishes he were dead or any thoughts of possible death to self
    3= Suicidal ideas or gesture
    4= Attempts at suicide (any serious attempt rates 4)

4. INSOMNIA EARLY

———

    0= No difficulty falling asleep
    1= Complains of occasional difficulty falling asleep—i.e., more than 1/2 hour
    2= Complains of nightly difficulty falling asleep

5. INSOMNIA MIDDLE

———

    0= No difficulty
    1= Patient complains of being restless and disturbed during the night
    2= Waking during the night—any getting out of bed rates 2 (except for purposes of voiding)

---

6. **INSOMNIA LATE**

_____

0= No difficulty
1= Waking in early hours of the morning but goes back to sleep
2= Unable to fall asleep again if he gets out of bed

7. **WORK AND ACTIVITIES**

_____

0= No difficulty
1= Thoughts and feelings of incapacity, fatigue or weakness related to activities; work or hobbies
2= Loss of interest in activity; hobbies or work—either directly reported by patient, or indirect in listlessness, indecision and vacillation (feels he has to push self to work or activities)
3= Decrease in actual time spent in activities or decrease in productivity
4= Stopped working because of present illness

8. **RETARDATION: PSYCHOMOTOR** (Slowness of thought and speech; impaired ability to concentrate; decreased motor activity)

_____

0= Normal speech and thought
1= Slight retardation at interview
2= Obvious retardation at interview
3= Interview difficult
4= Complete stupor

9. **AGITATION**

_____

0= None
1= Fidgetiness
2= Playing with hands, hair, etc.
3= Moving about, can't sit still
4= Hand wringing, nail biting, hair-pulling, biting of lips

10. **ANXIETY (PSYCHOLOGICAL)**

_____

0= No difficulty
1= Subjective tension and irritability
2= Worrying about minor matters
3= Apprehensive attitude apparent in face or speech
4= Fears expressed without questioning

11. **ANXIETY SOMATIC:** Physiological concomitants of anxiety, (i.e., effects of autonomic overactivity, "butterflies," indigestion, stomach cramps, belching, diarrhea, palpitations, hyperventilation, paresthesia, sweating, flushing, tremor, headache, urinary frequency). Avoid asking about possible medication side effects (i.e., dry mouth, constipation)

_____

0= Absent
1= Mild
2= Moderate
3= Severe
4= Incapacitating

12. SOMATIC SYMPTOMS (GASTROINTESTINAL)

0= None
1= Loss of appetite but eating without encouragement from others. Food intake about normal
2= Difficulty eating without urging from others. Marked reduction of appetite and food intake

13. SOMATIC SYMPTOMS GENERAL

0= None
1= Heaviness in limbs, back or head. Backaches, headache, muscle aches. Loss of energy and fatigability
2= Any clear-cut symptom rates 2

14. GENITAL SYMPTOMS (Symptoms such as: loss of libido; impaired sexual performance; menstrual disturbances)

0= Absent
1= Mild
2= Severe

15. HYPOCHONDRIASIS

0= Not present
1= Self-absorption (bodily)
2= Preoccupation with health
3= Frequent complaints, requests for help, etc.
4= Hypochondriacal delusions

16. LOSS OF WEIGHT

A. When rating by history:
  0= No weight loss
  1= Probably weight loss associated with present illness
  2= Definite (according to patient) weight loss
  3= Not assessed

17. INSIGHT

0= Acknowledges being depressed and ill
1= Acknowledges illness but attributes cause to bad food, climate, overwork, virus, need for rest, etc.
2= Denies being ill at all

18. DIURNAL VARIATION

A. Note whether symptoms are worse in morning or evening. If NO diurnal variation, mark none
  0= No variation
  1= Worse in A.M.
  2= Worse in P.M.
B. When present, mark the severity of the variation. Mark "None" if NO variation
  0= None
  1= Mild
  2= Severe

----

19. **DEPERSONALIZATION AND DEREALIZATION** (Such as: Feelings of unreality; Nihilistic ideas)

_____

0= Absent
1= Mild
2= Moderate
3= Severe
4= Incapacitating

20. **PARANOID SYMPTOMS**

_____

0= None
1= Suspicious
2= Ideas of reference
3= Delusions of reference and persecution

21. **OBSESSIONAL AND COMPULSIVE SYMPTOMS**

_____

0= Absent
1= Mild
2= Severe

Total Score _____

Appendix B

Interpersonal Psychotherapy Outcome Scale, Therapist's Version

Therapist _____ Patient _____ #_____
Date _____ Treatment phase completed: Acute _____ Continuation _____
To be completed at the end of the treatment phase:

1. The primary focus of this treatment was (check one):
   _____ grief (complicated bereavement) _____ role transition
   _____ role dispute   _____ interpersonal deficits
2. Secondary foci of treatment (check all addressed):
   _____ grief (complicated bereavement) _____ role transition
   _____ role dispute   _____ interpersonal deficits
3. *Regardless of the outcome of the depressive symptoms,* how much did the interpersonal problem areas change during the course of the treatment? Circle one number for each relevant treated area:

	Worsened significantly	Worsened slightly	No change	Improved slightly	Improved greatly
Grief	1	2	3	4	5
Role dispute	1	2	3	4	5
Role transition	1	2	3	4	5
Interpersonal deficits	1	2	3	4	5

Describe the changes: _____
_____
_____

(Version 1.0, 1/97)

References

Associated Manual References

Clougherty, K. F., Verdeli, H., & Weissman, M. M. (2003). Interpersonal psychotherapy adapted for a group in Uganda (IPT-G-U). Unpublished manual available from M. M. Weissman, New York State Psychiatric Institute, 1051 Riverside Drive, Unit 24, New York, NY 10032 (mmw3@columbia.edu).

Frank, E. (2005). *Treating bipolar disorder: A clinician's guide to interpersonal and social rhythm therapy.* New York: Guilford.

Hinrichsen, G. A., & Clougherty, K. F. (2006). Interpersonal psychotherapy for depressed older adults. Washington, DC: American Psychological Association.

Klerman, G. L., Weissman, M. M., Rounsaville, B., & Chevron, E. (1984). *Interpersonal psychotherapy of depression.* New York: Basic Books.

Lipsitz, J. D., & Markowitz, J. C. (2006). Manual for interpersonal psychotherapy for social phobia (IPT-SP). Unpublished manual available from Joshua D. Lipsitz, Ph.D., Anxiety Disorders Clinic, New York State Psychiatric Association, 1051 Riverside Drive, Unit 69, New York, NY 10032 (lipsitz@pi.cmpc.columbia.edu; 212–543–5417).

Markowitz, J. C. (1998). *Interpersonal psychotherapy for dysthymic disorder.* Washington, DC: American Psychiatric Publishing.

Mufson, L., Pollack Dorta, K., Moreau, D., & Weissman, M. M. (2004). *Interpersonal psychotherapy for depressed adolescents* (2d ed.). New York: Guilford.

Pilowsky, D., & Weissman, M. M. (2005). Interpersonal psychotherapy with school-aged depressed children. Unpublished manual available from Dan Pilowsky, Ph.D., 1051 Riverside Drive, Unit 24, New York, NY 10032 (Pilowskd@childpsych.columbia.edu).

Spinelli, M. G. (1999). Manual of interpersonal psychotherapy for antepartum depressed women (IPT-P). Unpublished manual, College of Physicians and Surgeons of Columbia University, New York State Psychiatric Institute, 1051 Riverside Drive, Box 123, New York, NY 10032.

Weissman, M. M. (2005). *Mastering depression through interpersonal psychotherapy: Monitoring forms.* New York: Oxford University Press.

Weissman, M. M., & Klerman, G. L. (1986). Interpersonal counseling (IPC) for stress and distress in primary care settings. Unpublished manual available through M. M. Weissman, Ph.D., 1051 Riverside Drive, Unit 24, New York, NY 10032 (mmw3@columbia.edu).

Weissman, M. M., Markowitz, J. C., & Klerman, G. L. (2000). *Comprehensive guide to interpersonal psychotherapy.* New York: Basic Books.

Wilfley, D. E., Mackenzie, K. R., Welch, R., Ayres, V., & Weissman, M. M. (Eds.). (2000). *Interpersonal psychotherapy for group.* New York: Basic Books.

Translations

French—Weissman, M. M., Markowitz, J. C., Klerman, G. L. (2006). *Guide de psychotherapie interpersonnelle* (S. Patry, Trans.). New York: Basic Books.

German—Shramm, E. (1996). *Interpersonelle Psychotherapie bei Depressionen und anderen psychischen Störungen.* New York: Schattauer.

Italian—Klerman, G. L., Weissman, M. M., Rounsaville, B. J., & Chevron, E. S. (1989). In G. Berti Ceroni (Ed.), *Psicoterapia interpersonale della depressione* (P. Galezzi, Trans.). Torino, Italy: Bollati Boringhieri.

Japanese—Klerman, G. L., Weissman, M. M., Rounsaville, B. J., & Chevron, E. S. (1997). *Interpersonal psychotherapy of depression.* (H. Mizushima, M. Shimada, and Y. Ono, Trans.). Tokyo: Iwasaki Gakujyutsa.

Works Cited

Agras, W. S., Walsh, T., Fairburn, C. G., Wilson, G. T., & Kraemer, H. C. (2000). A multicenter comparison of cognitive-behavioral therapy and interpersonal psychotherapy for bulimia nervosa. *Archives of General Psychiatry, 57,* 459–466.

Alem, A., Destal, M., & Araya, M. (August 1995). Mental health in Ethiopia: EPHA expert group report. *Ethiopian Journal of Health Development, 9*(1).

Alexopoulos, G. S., Katz, I. R., Bruce, M. L., Heo, M., Have, T. T., Raue, P., et al. (2005). Remission in depressed geriatric primary care patients: A report from the PROSPECT Study. *American Journal of Psychiatry, 162,* 718–724.

American Psychiatric Association. (1994). *Diagnostic and statistical manual for mental disorders,* 4th ed. Washington, DC: American Psychiatric Association.

American Psychiatric Association, & Rush, A. J., Jr. (2000). *Handbook of psychiatric measures.* Washington, DC: American Psychiatric Association.

Angus, L., & Gillies, L. A. (1994). Counseling the borderline client: An interpersonal approach. *Canadian Journal of Counseling/Rev Can de Counsel, 28,* 69–82.

APA Working Group on the Older Adult. (1998). What practitioners should know about working with older adults. *Professional Psychology: Research and Practice, 29,* 413–427.

Arbuckle, T. Y., Nohara-LeClair, M., & Pushkar, D. (2000). Effect of off-target verbosity on communication efficiency in a referential communication task. *Psychology and Aging, 15,* 65–77.

Barber, J. P., & Muenz, L. R. (1996). The role of avoidance and obsessiveness in matching patients to cognitive and interpersonal psychotherapy: Empirical findings from the treatment for depression collaborative research program. *Journal of Consulting and Clinical Psychology, 64,* 951–958.

Bateman, A., & Fonagy, P. (2001). Treatment of borderline personality disorder with psychoanalytically oriented partial hospitalization: An 18-month follow-up. *American Journal of Psychiatry, 158,* 36–42.

Bleiberg, K. L., & Markowitz, J. C. (2005). Interpersonal psychotherapy for posttraumatic stress disorder. *American Journal of Psychiatry, 162,* 181–183.

Blom, M. B. J., Hoencamp, E., & Zwaan, T. (1996). Interpersoonlijke psychotherapie voor depressie: Een pilot-onderzoek. *Tijdschrift voor Psychiatr, 38,* 398–402.

Bolton, P., Bass, J., Neugebauer, R., Verdeli, H., Clougherty, K. F., Wickramaratne, P., et al. (2003). Group interpersonal psychotherapy for depression in rural Uganda: A randomized controlled trial. *Journal of the American Medical Association, 289,* 3117–3124.

Brody, A. L., Saxena, S., Stoessel, P., Gillies, L. A., Fairbanks, L. A., Alborzian, S., et al. (2001). Regional brain metabolic changes in patients with major depression treated with either paroxetine or interpersonal psychotherapy: Preliminary findings. *Archives of General Psychiatry, 58,* 631–640.

Browne, G., Steiner, M., Roberts, J., Gafni, A., Byrne, C., Dunn, E., et al. (2002). Sertraline and/or interpersonal psychotherapy for patients with dysthymic disorder in primary care: 6–month comparison with longitudinal 2-year follow-up of effectiveness and costs. *Journal of Affecive Disorders, 68,* 317–330.

Bruce, M. L., Have, T. T., Reynolds, C. F., Katz, I. I., Schulberg, H. C., Mulsant, B. H., et al. (2004). Reducing suicidal ideation and depressive symptoms in depressed older primary care patients: A randomized controlled trial. *Journal of the American Medical Association, 291,* 1081–1091.

Caron, A., & Weissman, M. M. (2006). Interpersonal psychotherapy for the treatment of depression in medical patients. *Primary Psychiatry, 13*(5): 43–50.

Carroll, K. M., Rounsaville, B. J., & Gawin, F. H. (1991). A comparative trial of psychotherapies for ambulatory cocaine abusers: Relapse prevention and interpersonal psychotherapy. *American Journal of Drug and Alcohol Abuse, 17,* 229–247.

Caspi, A., Sugden, K., Moffitt, T. E., Taylor, A., Craig, I. W., Harrington, H., et al. (2003). Influence of life stress on depression: Moderation by a polymorphism in the 5-HTT gene. *Science, 18,* 386–389.

Cherry, S., & Markowitz, J. C. (1996). Interpersonal psychotherapy. In J. S. Kantor (Ed.), *Clinical depression during addiction recovery: Process, diagnosis, and treatment* (165–185). New York: Marcel Dekker.

Clougherty, K. F., Verdeli, H., & Weissman, M. M. (2003). Interpersonal psychotherapy adapted for a group in Uganda (IPT-G-U). Unpublished manual available through M. M. Weissman, New York State Psychiatric Institute, 1051 Riverside Drive, Unit 24, New York, NY 10032 (mmw3@columbia.edu).

Cohen, L. S., Altshuler, L. L., Harlow, B. L., Nonacs, R., Newport, D. J., Viguera, A. C., et al. (2006). Relapse of major depression during pregnancy in women who maintain or discontinue antidepressant treatment. *Journal of the American Medical Association, 295,* 499–507.

Cyranowski, J. M., Frank, E., Winter, E., Rucci, P., Novick, D., Pilkonis, P., et al. (2004). Personality pathology and outcome in recurrently depressed women over 2 years of maintenance interpersonal psychotherapy. *Psychological Medicine, 34,* 659–669.

Davis, D., Thomson O'Brien, M. A., Freemantle, N., Wolf, F. M., Mazmanian, P., & Taylor-Vaisey, A. (1999). Impact of formal continuing medical education: Do conferences, workshops, rounds, and other formal traditional continuing education activities change physician behavior and health care outcomes? *Journal of the American Medical Association, 282,* 867–874.

Donnelly, J. M., Kornblith, A. B., Fleishman, S., Zuckerman, E., Raptis, G., Hudis,

C. A., et al (2000). A pilot study of interpersonal psychotherapy by telephone with cancer patients and their partners. *Psycho-Oncology, 9,* 44–56.

Elkin, I., Shea, M. T., Watkins, J. T., Imber, S. D., Sotsky, S. M., Collins, J. F., et al. (1989). National Institute of Mental Health treatment of depression collaborative research program: General effectiveness of treatments. *Archives of General Psychiatry, 46,* 971–982.

Evans, D. L., Charney, D. S., Lewis, L., Golden, R. N., Gorman, J. M., Ranga Rama Krishnan, K., et al. (2005). Mood disorders in the medically ill: Scientific review and recommendations. *Biological Psychiatry, 58,* 175–189.

Fairburn, C. G., Jones, R., & Peveler, R. C. (1991).Three psychological treatments for bulimia nervosa: A comparative trial. *Archives of General Psychiatry, 48,* 463–469.

Fairburn, C. G., Jones, R., Peveler, R. C., Hope, R. A., & O'Connor, M. (1993). Psychotherapy and bulimia nervosa: Longer-term effects of interpersonal psychotherapy, behavior therapy, and cognitive behavior therapy. *Archives of General Psychiatry, 50,* 419–428.

Fairburn, C. G., Norman, P. A., Welch, S. L., O'Connor, M. E., Doll, H. A., & Peveler, R. C. (1995). A prospective study of outcome in bulimia nervosa and the long-term effects of three psychological treatments. *Archives of General Psychiatry, 52,* 304–312.

Feijò de Mello, M., Myczowisk, L. M., & Menezes, P. R. (2001). A randomized controlled trial comparing moclobemide and moclobemide plus interpersonal psychotherapy in the treatment of dysthymic disorder. *Journal of Psychotherapy Practice and Research, 10,* 117–123.

Foley, S. H., O'Malley, S., Rounsaville, B., Prusoff, B. A., & Weissman, M. M. (1987). The relationship of patient difficulty to therapist performance in interpersonal psychotherapy of depression. *Journal of Affective Disorders, 12,* 207–217.

Foley, S. H., Rounsaville, B. J., Weissman, M. M., Sholomskas, D., & Chevron, E. (1989). Individual versus conjoint interpersonal psychotherapy for depressed patients with marital disputes. *International Journal of Family Psychiatry,10,* 29–42.

Frank, E. (2005). *Treating bipolar disorder: A clinician's guide to interpersonal and social rhythm therapy.* New York: Guilford.

Frank, E., Kupfer, D. J., Perel, J. M., Cornes, C. D., Jarrett, B., Mallinger, A. G., et al. (1990). Three-year outcomes for maintenance therapies in recurrent depression. *Archives of General Psychiatry, 47,*1093–1099.

Frank, E., Kupfer, D. J., Thase, M. E., Mallinger, A. G., Swartz, H., Fagiolini, A. M., et al. (2005). Two-year outcomes for interpersonal and social rhythm therapy in individuals with bipolar I disorder. *Archives of General Psychiatry, 62,* 996–1004.

Frank, E., Kupfer, D. J., Wagner, E. F., McEachran, A. B., & Cornes, C. (1991). Efficacy of interpersonal psychotherapy as a maintenance treatment of recurrent depression: Contributing factors. *Archives of General Psychiatry, 48,* 1053–1059.

Frank, E., Swartz, H. A., & Kupfer, D. J. (2000). Interpersonal and social rhythm therapy: Managing the chaos of bipolar disorder. *Biological Psychiatry, 48,* 593–604.

Frank, J. (1971). Therapeutic factors in psychotherapy. *American Journal of Psychotherapy, 25,* 350–361.

Frasure-Smith, N., Koszycki, D., Swenson, J. R., Swenson, J. R., Baker, B., van Zyl,

L.T., et al. (2006). Design and rationale for a randomized, controlled trial of interpersonal psychotherapy and citalopram for depression in coronary artery disease. *Psychosomatic Medicine, 68,* 87–93.

Gallo, J. J., Bogner, H. R., Morales, K. H., Post, E. P., Have, T. T., & Bruce, M. L. (2005). Depression, cardiovascular disease, diabetes, and two-year mortality among older, primary-care patients. *American Journal of Geriatric Psychiatry, 13,* 748–755.

Grote, N. K., Bledsoe, S. E., Swartz, H.A., & Frank, E. (2004). Feasibility of providing culturally relevant, brief interpersonal psychotherapy for antenatal depression in an obstetrics clinic: A pilot study. *Research on Social Work Practice, 14,* 397–407.

Hamilton, M. (1960). A rating scale for depression. *Journal of Neurology, Neurosurgery, and Psychiatry, 25,* 56–62.

Hellerstein, D. J., Little, S. A. S., Samstag, L. W., Batchelder, S., Muran, J. C., Fedak, M., et al. (2001). Adding group psychotherapy to medication treatment in dysthymia. *Journal of Psychotherapy Practice and Research, 10,* 93–103.

Hinrichsen, G. A., & Clougherty, K. F. (2006). *Interpersonal psychotherapy for depressed older adults.* Washington, DC: American Psychological Association.

Hoffart, A. (2005). Interpersonal therapy for social phobia: Theoretical model and review of the evidence. In M. E. Abelian (Ed.), *Focus on psychotherapy research* (pp. 4–11). New York: Nova Science.

Judd, F. K., Piterman, L., Cockram, A. M., McCall, L., & Weissman, M. M. (2001). A comparative study of venlafaxine with a focused education and psychotherapy program versus venlafaxine alone in the treatment of depression in general practice. *Human Psychopharmacology 6,* 423–428.

Judd, F. K., Weissman, M. M., Davis, J., Hodgins, G., & Piterman, L. (2004). Interpersonal counseling in general practice. *Australian Family Physician, 33,* 332–337.

Judd, L. L., & Akiskal, H. S. (2000). Delineating the longitudinal structure of depressive illness: Beyond clinical subtypes and duration thresholds. *Pharmacopsychiatry, 1,* 3–7.

Judd, L. L., Akiskal, H. S., Maser, J. D., Zeller, P. J., Endicott, J., Coryell, W., et al. (1998). A prospective 12–year study of subsyndromal and syndromal depressive symptoms in unipolar major depressive disorders. *Archives of General Psychiatry, 55,* 694–700.

Karp, J. F., Scott, J., Houck, P., Reynolds, C. F., III, Kupfer, D. J., & Frank, E. (2005). Pain predicts longer time to remission during treatment of recurrent depression. *Journal of Clinical Psychiatry, 66,* 591–597.

Kebede, D., & Alem, A. (1999). Major mental disorders in Addis Ababa, Ethiopia, II: Affective disorders. *ACTA Paediatrica Scandinaica Supplement, 397,* 18–23.

Klerman, G. L., Budman, S., Berwick, D., Weissman, M. M., Damico-White, J., Demby, A., et al. (1987). Efficacy of a brief psychosocial intervention for symptoms of stress and distress among patients in primary care. *Medical Care, 25,* 1078–1088.

Klerman, G. L., DiMascio, A., Weissman, M. M., Prusoff, B. A., & Paykel, E. S. (1974). Treatment of depression by drugs and psychotherapy. *American Journal of Psychiatry, 131,* 186–191.

Klerman, G. L., Weissman, M. M., Rounsaville, B., & Chevron, E. (1984). *Interpersonal psychotherapy of depression.* New York: Basic Books.

Koszycki, D., Lafontaine, S., Frasure-Smith, N., Swenson, R., & Lesperance, F. (2004). An open-label trial of interpersonal psychotherapy in depressed patients with coronary disease. *Psychosomatics, 45,* 319–324.

Krupnick, J. L. (1999). Interpersonal psychotherapy for PTSD following interpersonal trauma. Presentation at symposium on New Developments in Interpersonal Psychotherapy (J. C. Markowitz, chair). American Psychiatric Association Annual Meeting, Washington, DC, May 17.

Lichtmacher, J. E., Eisendrath, S. J., & Haller, E. (2006). Implementing interpersonal psychotherapy into a psychiatry residency training program. *Academic Psychiatry, 30,* 385–391.

Linehan, M. M., Armstrong, H. E., Suárez, A., Allmon, D., & Heard, H. L. (1991). Cognitive-behavioral treatment of chronically parasuicidal borderline patients. *Archives of General Psychiatry, 48,* 1060–1064.

Lipsitz, J. D., Fyer, A. J., Markowitz, J. C., & Cherry, S. (1999). An open trial of interpersonal psychotherapy for social phobia. *American Journal of Psychiatry, 156,* 1814–1816.

Lipsitz, J. D., Gur, M., Miller, N., Vermes, D., & Fyer, A. J. (2006). An open trial of interpersonal psychotherapy for panic disorder (IPT-PD). *Journal of Nervous and Mental Disease, 194*(6): 440–445.

Lipsitz, J. D., & Markowitz, J. C. (2006). Manual for interpersonal psychotherapy for social phobia (IPT-SP). Available from Joshua D. Lipsitz, Ph.D., Anxiety Disorders Clinic, New York State Psychiatric Association, 1051 Riverside Drive, Unit 69, New York, NY 10032 (lipsitz@pi.cmpc.columbia.edu; 212–543–5417).

Lo, H. T., & Fung, K. (2003). Culturally Competent Psychotherapy. *Canadian Journal of Psychiatry, 48,* 161–170.

Markowitz, J. C. (1993). Psychotherapy of the postdysthymic patient. *Journal of Psychotherapy Practice and Research, 2,* 157–163.

Markowitz, J. C. (1998). *Interpersonal psychotherapy of dysthymic disorder.* Washington, DC: American Psychiatric Press.

Markowitz, J. C. (2005). Interpersonal therapy of personality disorders. In J. M. Oldham, A. E. Skodol, & D. E. Bender (Eds.), *Textbook of personality disorders* (pp. 321–338). Washington, DC: American Psychiatric Publishing.

Markowitz, J. C., Bleiberg, K. L., Christos, P., & Levitan, E. (2006). Solving interpersonal problems correlates with symptom improvement in interpersonal psychotherapy: Preliminary findings. *Journal of Nervous and Mental Disease, 194,* 15–20.

Markowitz, J. C., Kocsis, J. H., Bleiberg, K. L., Christos, P. J., & Sacks, M. H. (2005). A comparative trial of psychotherapy and pharmacotherapy for "pure" dysthymic patients. *Journal of Affective Disorders, 89,* 167–175.

Markowitz, J. C., Kocsis, J. H., Fishman, B., Spielman, L. A., Jacobsberg, L. B., Frances, A. J., et al. (1998). Treatment of HIV-positive patients with depressive symptoms. *Archives of General Psychiatry, 55,* 452–457.

Markowitz, J. C., Leon, A. C., Miller, N. L., Cherry, S., Clougherty, K. F., & Villalobos, L. (2000). Rater agreement on interpersonal psychotherapy problem areas. *Journal of Psychotherapy Practice and Research, 9,*131–135.

Markowitz, J. C., Skodol, A. E., & Bleiberg, K. (2006). Interpersonal psychotherapy for borderline personality disorder: Possible mechanisms of change. *Journal of Clinical Psychology, 62,* 431–444.

Markowitz, J. C., Svartberg, M., & Swartz, H. A. (1998). Is IPT time-limited psychodynamic psychotherapy? *Journal of Psychotherapy Practice and Research, 7,* 185–195.

Markowitz, J. C., & Swartz, H. A. (1997). Case formulation in interpersonal psychotherapy of depression. In T. D. Eells (Ed.), *Handbook of psychotherapy case formulation* (pp. 192–222). New York: Guilford.

Markowitz, J. C., & Swartz, H. A. (2006). Case formulation in interpersonal psychotherapy of depression. In *Handbook of psychotherapy case formulation.* (2d ed.) New York: Guilford. Nov.

Martin, S. D., Martin, E., Rai, S. S., Richardson, M. A., & Royall, R. (2001). Brain blood flow changes in depressed patients treated with interpersonal psychotherapy or venlafaxine hydrochloride. *Archives of General Psychiatry, 58,* 641–648.

McIntosh, V. V., Jordan, J., Carter, F. A., Luty, S. E., McKenzie, J.M., Bulik, C. M., et al. (2005). Three psychotherapies for anorexia nervosa: A randomized, controlled trial. *American Journal of Psychiatry, 162,* 741–747.

Miller, G. (2006). The unseen: Mental illness's global toll. *Science, 311,* 458–465.

Miller, L., & Weissman, M. M. (2002). Interpersonal psychotherapy delivered over the telephone to recurrent depressives: A pilot study. *Depression and Anxiety, 16,* 114–117.

Miller, M. D., Richards, V., Zuckoff, A., Martire, L. M., Morse, J., Frank, E., et al. (2006). A model for modifying interpersonal psychotherapy (IPT) for depressed elders with cognitive impairment. *Clinical Gerontology.* Dec.

Mossey, J. M., Knott, K. A., Higgins, M., & Talerico, K. (1996). Effectiveness of a psychosocial intervention, interpersonal counseling, for subdysthymic depression in medically ill elderly. *Journal of Gerontology Series A: Biological Sciences and Medical Sciences, 51A,* M172–M178.

Mufson, L., Pollack Dorta, K., Moreau, D., & Weissman, M. M. (2004*).* *Interpersonal psychotherapy for depressed adolescents* (2d ed.). New York: Guilford.

Mufson, L., Pollack Dorta, K., Wickramaratne, P., Nomura, Y., Olfson, M., & Weissman, M. M. (2004). A randomized effectiveness trial of interpersonal psychotherapy for depressed adolescents. *Archives of General Psychiatry, 61,* 577–583.

Neugebauer, R., Kline, J., Bleiberg, K., Baxi, L., Markowitz, J.C., Rosing, M., et al. (in press). Preliminary open trial of interpersonal counseling for subsyndromal depression following miscarriage. *Depression and Anxiety.*

Neugebauer, R., Kline, J., Markowitz, J.C., Bleiberg, K., Baxi, L., Rosing, M., et al. (2006). Pilot randomized controlled trial of interpersonal counseling for subsyndromal depression following miscarriage. *Journal of Clinical Psychiatry, 67,* 1299–1304.

Novalis, P. N., Rojcewicz, S. J., & Peele, R. (1993). *Clinical manual of supportive psychotherapy.* Washington, DC: American Psychiatric Press.

O'Hara, M. W., Stuart, S, Gorman, L. L., & Wenzel, A. (2000). Efficacy of interpersonal psychotherapy for postpartum depression. *Archives of General Psychiatry, 57,* 1039–1045.

Pilowsky, D., & Weissman, M. M. (2005). Interpersonal psychotherapy with school-aged depressed children. Unpublished manual available from Dan Pilowsky, MD, 1051 Riverside Drive, Unit 24, New York, NY 10032 (Pilowskd@childpsych .columbia.edu).

Pinsker, H. (1997). *A primer of supportive psychotherapy.* Hillsdale, NJ: Analytic Press.

Reynolds, C. F., III, Dew, M. A., Pollock, B. G., Mulsant, B. H., Frank, E., Miller, M. D., et al. (2006). Maintenance treatment of major depression in old age. *New England Journal of Medicine, 354,* 1130–1138.

Reynolds, C. F., III, Frank, E., Dew, M. A., Houck, P. R., Miller, M., Mazumdar, S., et al. (1999). Treatment of 70(+)-year-olds with recurrent major depression: Excellent short-term but brittle long-term response. *American Journal of Geriatric Psychiatry, 7,* 64–69.

Reynolds, C. F., III, Frank, E., Perel, J. M., Imber, S. D., Cornes, C., Miller, M. D., et al. (1999). Nortriptyline and interpersonal psychotherapy as maintenance therapies for recurrent major depression: A randomized controlled trial in patients older than fifty-nine years. *Journal of the American Medical Association, 281,* 39–45.

Robertson, M., Rushton, P. J., Bartrum, D., & Ray, R. (2004). Group-based interpersonal psychotherapy for posttraumatic stress disorder: Theoretical and clinical aspects. *International Journal of Group Psychotherapy, 54,* 145–175.

Rossello, J., & Bernal, G. (1999). The efficacy of cognitive-behavioral and interpersonal treatments for depression in Puerto Rican adolescents. *Journal of Consulting and Clinical Psychology, 67,* 734–745.

Rounsaville, B. J., Chevron, E. S., Weissman, M. M., Prusoff, B. A., & Frank, E. (1986). Training therapists to perform interpersonal psychotherapy in clinical trials. *Comprehensive Psychiatry, 27,* 364–371.

Rounsaville, B. J., Glazer, W., Wilber, C. H., Weissman, M. M., & Kleber, H. D. (1983). Short-term interpersonal psychotherapy in methadone-maintained opiate addicts. *Archives of General Psychiatry, 40,* 629–636.

Schulberg, H. C., Post, E. P., Raue, P. J., Have, T. T., Miller, M., & Bruce, M. L. (in press). Treating late-life depression with interpersonal psychotherapy in the primary care sector. *International Journal of Geriatric Psychiatry.*

Schulberg, H. C., Raue, P. J., & Rollman, B. L. (2002). The effectiveness of psychotherapy in treating depressive disorders in primary care practice: clinical and cost perspectives. *General Hospital Psychiatry, 24,* 203–212.

Scocco, P., & Frank, E. (2002). Interpersonal psychotherapy as augmentation treatment in depressed elderly responding poorly to antidepressant drugs: A case series. *Psychotherapy and Psychosomatics, 71,* 357–361.

Scogin, F., & McElreath, I. (1994). Efficacy of psychosocial treatments for geriatric depression: A quantitative review. *Journal of Consulting and Clinical Psychology, 57,* 403–407.

Shea, M. T., Sout, R., Gunderson, J., Morey, L. C., Grilo, C. M., McGlashan, T., et al. (2002). Short-term diagnostic stability of schizotypal, borderline, avoidant, and obsessive-compulsive personality disorders. *American Journal of Psychiatry, 159,* 2036–2040.

Shear, K., Frank, E., Houck, P., & Reynolds, C. F. (2005). Treatment of complicated grief: A randomized controlled trial. *Journal of the American Medical Association, 293,* 2601–2608.

Spinelli, M. G. (1999). Manual of interpersonal psychotherapy for antepartum depressed women (IPT-P). Unpublished manual, College of Physicians and Surgeons of Columbia University, New York State Psychiatric Institute, 1051 Riverside Drive, Box 123, New York, NY 10032.

Spinelli, M. G., & Endicott, J. (2003). Controlled clinical trial of interpersonal psychotherapy versus parenting education program for depressed pregnant women. *American Journal of Psychiatry, 160,* 555–562.

Stuart, S., & Noyes, R., Jr. (in press). Interpersonal psychotherapy for somatizing patients. *Psychotherapy and Psychosomatics, 75.*

Verdeli, H., Clougherty, K. F., Bolton, P., Speelman, L., Ndogoni, L., Bass, J., et al. (2003). Adapting group interpersonal psychotherapy for a developing country: experience in rural Uganda. *World Psychiatry, 2,* 114–120.

Weissman, M. M. (2005). *Mastering depression through interpersonal psychotherapy: Monitoring forms.* New York: Oxford University Press.

Weissman, M. M. (2006). A brief history of Interpersonal Psychotherapy. *Psychiatric Annals, 36,* 553–557.

Weissman, M. M., & Klerman, G. L. (1986). Interpersonal counseling (IPC) for stress and distress in primary care settings. Unpublished manual available through M. M. Weissman, Ph.D., 1051 Riverside Drive, Unit 24, New York, NY 10032 (mmw3@columbia.edu).

Weissman, M. M., Klerman, G. L., Prusoff, B. A., Sholomskas, D., & Padian, N. (1981). Depressed outpatients: Results one year after treatment with drugs and/ or interpersonal psychotherapy. *Archives of General Psychiatry, 38,* 52–55.

Weissman, M. M., Markowitz, J. C., & Klerman, G. L. (2000). *Comprehensive guide to interpersonal psychotherapy.* New York: Basic Books.

Weissman, M. M., Pilowsky, D. J., Wickramaratne, P., Talati, A., Wisniewski, S. R., Fava, M., et al. (2006). Remission of maternal depression is associated with reductions in psychopathology in their children: A Star*D-child report. *Journal of the American Medical Association, 295,* 1389–1398.

Weissman, M. M., Verdeli, H., Gameroff, M. J., Bledsoe, S. E., Betts, K., Mufson, L., et al. (2006). A national survey of psychotherapy training in psychiatry, psychology, and social work. *Archives of General Psychiatry, 63,* 925–934.

Weissman, M. M., Wolk, S., Goldstein, R. B., Moreau, D., Adams, P., Greenwald, S., et al. (1999). Depressed adolescents grown up. *Journal of the American Medical Association, 281,* 1707–1713.

Wilfley, D. E., Agras, W. S., Telch, C. F., Rossiter, E., Schneider, J., Cole, A. C., et al. (1993). Group cognitive-behavioral therapy and group interpersonal psychotherapy for the nonpurging bulimic individual: A controlled comparison. *Journal of Consulting and Clinical Psychology, 61,* 296–305.

Wilfley, D. E., Mackenzie, K. R., Welch, R., Ayres, V., & Weissman, M. M. (Eds.). (2000). *Interpersonal psychotherapy for group.* New York: Basic Books.

Wilfley, D. E., Welch, R. R., Stein, R. I., Spurrell, E. B., Cohen, L. R., Saelens, B. E., et al. (2002). A randomized comparison of group cognitive-behavioral therapy and group interpersonal psychotherapy for the treatment of overweight individuals with binge-eating disorder. *Archives of General Psychiatry, 59*(8), 713–721.

Zlotnick, C., Johnson, S. L., Miller, I. W., Pearlstein, T., & Howard, M. (2001). Postpartum depression in women receiving public assistance: Pilot study of an interpersonal-therapy-oriented group intervention. *American Journal of Psychiatry, 158,* 638–640.

Zuckerman, D. M., Prusoff, B. A., Weissman, M. M., & Padian, N.S. (1980). Personality as a predictor of psychotherapy and pharmacotherapy outcome for depressed outpatients. *Journal of Consulting and Clinical Psychology, 48,* 730–735.

Index

adolescent depression, 80–81, 98–102
affect, encouragement of, 64–65
  See also feelings, expressing
alcohol abuse, 17, 81, 129–131,
    144
anger, 39, 64–65, 112–113, 120, 142–
    145
  See also feelings, expressing
anorexia nervosa, 132–133
anxiety disorders, 136–141
assessment process. *See* symptoms,
    generally
Axis I *vs.* Axis II focus, 69–71

behavioral therapy, bipolar disorder,
    123–126
biology of depression, 80
bipolar disorder, 11, 123–126
Bleiberg, K. L., 139, 143
borderline personality disorder (BPD),
    69, 142–145
bulimia nervosa, 132–135, 157–158

cardiovascular disease, 110
case examples
  bipolar disorder, 125–126
  borderline personality disorder, 144–
    145
  dysthymic disorder, 120–122
  eating disorder, 133–135
  grief, 35–36, 64
  interpersonal deficits, 56–58
  interpersonal dispute, 42
  maintenance, 91–93
  medical patient, 112–114

older adult, 108–109
posttraumatic stress, 139–140
role transitions, 46–50, 64
social phobia, 137–139
catharsis process. *See* mourning process
CBT (cognitive behavior therapy), 71,
    76, 89, 132–133, 136
checklists and questionnaires
  grief reactions, 31–32
  Hamilton Rating Scale, 13, 60–61, 75,
    163–166
  interpersonal deficits, 54–55
  interpersonal disputes, 40
  interpersonal inventory, 22
  Outcome Scale, 167
  role transitions, 45
  Social Rhythm Metric, 124, 126
  symptom, 13–17
Cherry, S., 137
children and depression, 80–81, 98,
    102–103
chronic IPT model, 118–120
clarification, as technique, 65
clinical supervision, 162
cocaine addiction, 129–131
cognitive behavior therapy (CBT), 71,
    76, 89, 132–133, 136
cognitively-impaired patients, 107–
    108
Cohen, L. S., 94
communication analysis, 65–66
complicated grief. *See* grief
complicated pregnancy, 97
confidentiality, 78, 99–100, 152,
    159

conjoint IPT, 78, 159

contracts, treatment, xiii, 24–25, 59, 73–74

couples IPT, 78, 158–159

credentials, therapist, 77

crying, 33–34

cultural adaptations
Ethiopian experience, 154–156
principles of, 149–151
Ugandan experience, 151–154

decision analysis, 66

delusional depression, 10

depression
adolescents and children, 80–81, 98–102

depression, overview
diagnosis process, 12–18
explaining, 18–19, 23–25, 82
in ITP perspective, 3–6, 80–81
recurrence of, 82–83
sadness compared, 60
types of, 8–11
*See also specific problem areas, e.g., grief;
pregnancy; role transitions*

diabetes, in medical patient case example, 112–114

diagnosis process
generally, xii–xiii, 12–18
explaining, 18–19, 23–25, 82
grief reactions, 29–30, 31–32, 35–36

direct elicitation, 63–64

directive techniques, generally, 67

disputes, interpersonal, 37–42, 150, 153

dissolution, in interpersonal disputes, 38

double depression, 116, 117

drug abuse, 17, 81, 129–131, 144

DSM-IV criteria, major depressive order, 18

dysthymic disorder, 10–11, 116–122

eating disorders, 132–135

elderly adults, depression, 104–109

elicitation, direct, 63–64

emotions. *See* feelings, expressing

encouragement of affect. *See* feelings, expressing

Ethiopia, IPT adaptation, 154–156

Fairburn, C. G., 132–133

family involvement
generally, 28, 78
adolescent and child patients, 99–100, 101, 102–103
medical patients, 111–112
pregnant patients, 96

feelings, expressing
generally, 64–66, 67, 71–73, 74–75
in bipolar disorder case example, 125–126
in borderline personality disorder case example, 144–145
bulimia patients, 133, 134
dysthymic disorder, 119, 120–121
grief reactions, 30, 33–34
interpersonal deficits, 53, 56, 57–58
interpersonal disputes, 39, 41
in social phobia case example, 138
transgression label, 72, 119
Ugandan experience, 152, 153

focal area
and group IPT, 157, 158
identifying, xiii, 20–23
maintaining, 73, 107

formulation, presenting, xii–xiii, 18–19, 23–24, 119

Frank, E., 94, 123–124

Fryer, A. J., 137, 140

genotype and phenotype, 6

goals of treatment
generally, xiii, 6–7
bipolar disorder, 125
borderline personality disorder, 143
dysthymic disorder, 118–119
grief reactions, 30, 33
interpersonal deficits, 52–53
interpersonal disputes, 38–42
maintenance, 90–91
role transitions, 44–46, 47–48

grief
in bipolar disorder, 125
in case example, 35–36, 64
cultural context, 151, 153
IPT approach generally, 29–35
older adults, 106, 108–109
postpartum patients, 97

group IPT, 151–154, 157–158
Gur, M., 140

Hamilton Rating Scale, 13, 60–61, 75, 163–166
HIV infection, 110, 111, 112, 151
Holland, IPT adaptation, 154

iatrogenic role transition, 118–120, 137
impasse, in interpersonal disputes, 38
initial sessions
    overview, xii–xiii
    adolescents, 100
    alcohol and drug use, 81
    conjoint IPT, 159
    diagnosis explanations, 18–19
    eating disorders, 157
    formulation presentation, 23–24
    interpersonal inventory, 20–23
    medical patients, 112
    medication evaluation, 19–20
    sick role assignment, 25–26
    symptom assessment, 12–18
    telephone IPT, 159, 160
    treatment contract, 24–25
    Ugandan experience, 152
intellectualizing patients, 72–73
intermediate sessions, overview, xiii–xiv, 26–28
International Society for Interpersonal Psychotherapy, 149, 162
Interpersonal and Social Rhythm Therapy (IPSRT), 123–124, 126
interpersonal counseling (IPC), 111, 114–115
interpersonal deficits
    case example, 56–58
    cultural context issues, 151
    eating disorders, 157
    elderly patients, 106
    IPT approach generally, 51–56, 67
    pregnant patients, 97
    and substance abuse, 130
interpersonal disputes
    in bipolar disorder case example, 125–126
    case example, 42
    cultural context issues, 150, 151, 153

elderly patients, 106
IPT approach generally, 37–42
in maintenance case example, 92–93
passive patients, 71–72
postpartum patients, 97
and role transitions, 50
in social phobia case example, 138
and therapeutic relationship, 67
interpersonal inventory
    generally, xiii, 20–23
    adolescent patients, 100–101
    elderly patients, 107
    medical patients, 111
    pregnant patients, 95
interpersonal life, in depression, 5
interpersonal life, in therapy
    anxiety disorders, 136–141
    in borderline personality disorder case example, 144–145
    bulimia, 134–135
    grief reactions, 34–35
    role transitions, 46, 47, 48, 50
    See also interpersonal deficits;
        interpersonal disputes
interpersonal psychotherapy (IPT), overviews
    compared with other treatments, 71, 76–77
    cultural adaptations, 149–151
    and depression generally, 3–7, 8–11
    explaining to patient, 77
    family involvement, 78–79
    rating instruments, 163–167
    sessions in, ix–xiv
    techniques, 63–66
    therapist's role, xii–xiv, 6–8, 67–68
    See also symptoms, generally; *specific problem areas, e.g.,* grief; mood disorders; role transitions
IPC (interpersonal counseling), 111, 114–115
IPSRT (Interpersonal and Social Rhythm Therapy), 123–124, 126

Krupnick, J. L., 140

lateness to sessions, 74, 77–78
Lipsitz, J. D., 137, 140

maintenance treatment, 60–61, 89–93
major depressive order, 8, 9–11, 18, 89–
    93
    See also depression
mania, in bipolar disorder, 123–126
Markowitz, J. C., 137, 139, 143
medical model and older adults, 106–
    107
medical patients and depression, 104,
    110–115
medication
    alcohol and drug use, 81
    bipolar disorder, 123–124, 125
    dysthymic disorder, 117–118, 122
    elderly patients, 104, 105, 108
    and IPT generally, 4, 13, 19–20
    maintenance treatment, 89
    medical patients, 110
    pregnant and postpartum patients, 94–
        95
    termination phase evaluation, 59, 61
mild depression, 10
Miller, N., 140
miscarriage, 94–97
mood disorders, adaptation of IPT
    overview, 87–88
    adolescents and children, 98–103
    bipolar disorder, 123–126
    dysthymic disorder, 116–122
    maintenance treatment, 89–93
    medical patients, 110–115
    older adults, 104–109
    pregnant and postpartum patients, 94–
        97
Moreau, D., 101
mourning process
    grief, 30, 33–36, 97
    role transitions, 44, 46
Mufson, L., 101

Netherlands, IPT adaptation, 154
nicotine addiction, 129–131
nondirective exploration, 63
non-mood disorders, adaptation of IPT
    anxiety disorders, 136–141
    borderline personality disorder (BPD),
        69, 142–145
    eating disorders, 132–135
    substance abuse, 129–131

nonreciprocal expectations, 37
normal grief. *See* grief

older adults, depression, 89, 104–109
Outcome Scale, Interpersonal
    Psychotherapy, 167

panic disorder, 140–141
passive patients, 71–72
personality, in depression, 5
    See also sick role, assigning
personality disorder *vs.* psychiatric illness,
    69–71
Pilowsky, D., 102
Pollack Dorta, K., 101
postpartum depression, 94–97
posttraumatic stress disorder (PTSD), 35,
    139–140
pregnancy, 89, 94–97
problem area. *See* focal area
psychiatric illness *vs.* personality disorder,
    69–71
psychodynamic therapy, 76
psychotic depression, 10

questionnaires. *See* checklists and
    questionnaires
questions from patients, frequently asked,
    77–83

rating instruments. *See* checklists and
    questionnaires
Ravitz, Paula, 154–156
recording devices, 75–76
recurrence of depression, 82–83, 89–90,
    99
renegotiation, in interpersonal disputes,
    38, 39, 41–42
resources and training, 161–162
Reynolds, C. F., 105
role disputes. *See* interpersonal disputes
role-playing
    generally, 27–28, 66, 72
    in bipolar disorder case example, 125–
        126
    bulimia patients, 133
    dysthymic disorder, 119, 120
    in interpersonal deficits case example,
        58

in role transitions case example, 49
in social phobia case example, 138–139
role transitions
in bulimia case example, 134
case examples, 46–50, 64
cultural context issues, 151, 154
iatrogenic type, 118–120, 137
and interpersonal deficits, 57
and interpersonal disputes, 37
IPT approach generally, 43–46
in maintenance case example, 92
in medical patient case example, 113
medical patients, 111
older adults, 106
postpartum patients, 97
in posttraumatic stress case example, 140
substance abuse, 129, 130–131

sadness *vs.* depression, 60
self-disclosure, therapist's, 67
sick role, assigning
generally, xiii, 25–26, 70–71, 81
adolescent patients, 99
borderline personality disorder, 143
bulimia patients, 132–133
and group IPT, 157
medical patients, 112, 113
silence, 67–68, 74–75
Skodel, A. E., 143
social anxiety disorder, 136–139
social life. *See* interpersonal *entries*
social phobia, 136–139
Social Rhythm Metric (SRM), 124, 126
social support. *See* interpersonal *entries*
Spinelli, M. G., 97
SRM (Social Rhythm Metric), 124, 126
substance abuse, 17, 81, 129–131, 144
suicide
generally, 70, 82
adolescent patients, 98–99, 101–102
bipolar disorder, 123
borderline personality disorder, 144

elderly patients, 108
telephone IPT, 159, 160
supportive therapy, 76–77, 129–130, 131
symptoms, generally
in depression, 5
explaining, 18–19
IPT assessment process, 12–18, 61–62, 102–103
rating instruments, 75, 124, 126, 163–167
See also specific problem areas, e.g., grief; pregnancy; role transitions

techniques, interpersonal psychotherapy, 63–66
telephone sessions, 96, 99, 111, 143, 159–160
termination phase
generally, xiv, 59–62, 79–80, 89
borderline personality disorder, 144
Ugandan experience, 152
therapeutic relationship, as technique, 67–68
therapist's role, xii–xiv, 6–8, 33–34, 67–68
time limits
dysthymic disorder, 119–120
Ethiopian patients, 155
IPT generally, 24–25, 59, 73–74, 87
and maintenance treatment, 89–91
medical patients, 111, 112, 114–115
pregnant patients, 96
Toronto Addis Ababa Psychiatric Project (TAAPP), 154
training and resources, 161–162
transference, 67, 68
transgression label, 72, 119
treatment contracts, xiii, 24–25, 59, 73–74
treatment goals. *See* goals of treatment

Uganda, IPT adaptation, 151–154

Vermes, D., 140

Wilfley, D. E., 157
workshops, 161–162